MW01442087

Beautifully BROKEN

OUT OF THE ASHES I RISE

MARY AMA ZURUBA

Copyright © 2022 Mary Ama Zuruba

All rights reserved.

ISBN: 979-8-3745-2369-0

This book is a reflection of the author's current recollection of experiences and events over time. The names, characteristics, details and dialogues have been changed to preserve the anonymity or privacy of certain individuals, especially the guilty.

DEDICATION

I humbly dedicate this book to the Almighty God, my Father and Maker whose unmerited favor and grace have brought me this far and made this journey a reality. Indeed, with God, all things are possible.

I acknowledge my mother, Comfort Momba, for the sacrifices, commitment, dedication, love and unending support she provided me throughout the journey of my life. Obaatan pa Connie, may God continue to bless you with longevity embodied in good health. Thank you, Mama.

To my late father, Mr. Raphael Zuruba-Duke: thank you for the seed you planted in me. I am grateful for the previous time I had with you. Continue to rest peacefully in the bosom of your Maker. The seed God gave you, Daddy, landed on fertile grounds and God is still remaining faithful to His covenant. Rest on, my HERO, a man with a million-dollar smile.

To my children, Rachael, Sheila, David, and Destiny-Renee; thank you all for supporting me through all the seasons of my journey, which you have all become a part of. I love you all dearly.

To my siblings, Cynthia, Solomon, Victoria, and Kristina. Thank you for being a part of my life. Thank you for standing by my side through it all. You have always been my backbone and strong support. May God bless you.

To Mr. and Mrs. Amuzu; I thank you for obeying God's command and fulfilling the assignment of investing spiritually and emotionally in little Ama, who had no hope or shoulders to lean on. You gave me the precious gift of growing in the knowledge of the Lord. Your prayers, advice, and encouragement have not gone waste. I salute you.

To Dr. Mensa Otabil and the ICGC, I say thank you for your support in those challenging times, especially for supporting me through Secondary School. I could not have done it without you all. Papa, thank you. The seed you watered is blossoming to the glory of God.

To you my reading audience, as you read this book, I pray that God will restore and empower you!

CONTENTS

Dedication _____ iii
Acknowledgement _____ iv
Introduction _____ v
Chapter 1: Why Label Me? _____ 1
Chapter 2: Epitome of a Good Samaritan _____ 11
Chapter 3: Don't Squash my Dreams _____ 21
Chapter 4: Should You Really Quit? _____ 31
Chapter 5: A Great Heavenly Reward _____ 39
Chapter 6: Angels in Human Form _____ 49
Chapter 7: Don't be Quick to Judge Me _____ 57
Chapter 8: Dear Wayward Teen's Parent _____ 65
Chapter 9: Love Doesn't Have to be Blind _____ 73
Chapter 10: A Price for the Glory _____ 81
Chapter 11: Seeking Advancement _____ 89
Chapter 12: God's Master Plan _____ 99
Chapter 13: Evolve Again, Woman _____ 107
Chapter 14: The Cost of Greatness _____ 117
Epilogue _____ 125

INTRODUCTION

Out of the Ashes I Rise

Grace has many definitions, and I am one of them. My life from the 37 Military Barracks to Naugatuck, Connecticut in the United States of America is proof. Even more, the life of my mother from this same address to citizenship of the United States is further proof of the manifold grace of God.

This brief book is my testimony about the unmerited grace of God over my life. Grace that took me from the ashes of life to the pinnacle of glory and fulfillment. My life's trajectory is one that offers a million lessons I am convinced the world must hear.

My life has thought me what I think others should know, too. God has taught me that when we go through certain experiences in life, He may

INTRODUCTION

be telling us something crucial in the midst of it. He may be revealing something very important that requires us to remain sensitive to Him in order to catch the revelation. If we regard our circumstances carefully, we may be paying heed to His message, and thereby discover something significant—a life purpose or career or calling—in the midst of those trials and hardships and challenges. That is why it is important to try to get spiritual insight into what God is allowing on our life's journey. We have to seek God's face in the midst of our challenges in order to hear His message to us in our "mess".

Life does present opportunities for improving our lives and becoming better versions of ourselves. People who desire to see improvements in their lives and become better at their careers, calling or married lives must seize life's opportunities. They must take advantage of opportunities that come their way to achieve this end. We all have deep desires we wish to see come to pass. It is required that everyone dream big and follow their heart's desire. Bringing our lofty dreams to pass is possible because it is the responsibility of both ourselves and God—and with God, there is nothing impossible. It may not come to pass exactly as we planned, but God can make all things beautiful.

INTRODUCTION

God works according to times and seasons. People must learn still in their life storms until God comes through for them. The storms never last forever, and standing firm, we can overcome sooner than later. Keeping still while trusting in God, He will win our victories for us.

I have learned that in life, you will not always be paid well for the good you do. Sometimes, you can be paid evil for doing good to people. It is a part of life we must accept. If we desire rewards for the good we do, we should look up to God; He is the rewarder. Also, not every good thing we do in this life will be rewarded here on earth. Sometimes, our rewards are only in heaven.

Some people have the attitude of jumping to conclusions too quickly. They judge people and write them off quickly. I have learned not to be too quick to judge other people. I may not know why they do what they do. Rather than judge their actions, it should be my concern to help people change into better persons.

Love is an inevitable part of life, but many people approach it the wrong way. The most popular saying about love is that it is blind. "Love is blind", we often hear. But I have come to believe otherwise: Love doesn't have to be blind. To be

INTRODUCTION

blindly in love is to close one's eyes to negative character traits that can potentially lead to marital failure or stress in marriage in the future. One must not overlook danger signals in one's relationship because of love.

A lot of preparations are required before one enters the marriage institution. Begin well, and begin right. Let God lead you. Seek God's counsel in choosing your spouse. Preparing financially by making sure you have a job before deciding to settle. Be sure you are matured before entering into any relationship. Some people enter marriage in order to gain security. I have learned that it is the wrong approach as it could lure into a bad marriage.

When you get married, don't take advantage of your partner's vulnerability. You are each other's helpmate. Unite and be each other's keeper. Don't compete and fight between yourselves since you are one flesh. You can't love your neighbor more than yourself. So if you encounter abuse in your marriage, don't tolerate it; you could die through it.

If you decide to have children, give them the best care and support they will need in life. Pray for them even when they err or backslide. Don't

INTRODUCTION

curse them for going wayward or dragging your name into disrepute.

There is a price to pay for the glory. For the glory of God to manifest, we will sometimes have to pay the price of suffering for it. While my siblings and I were still young—the youngest aged only two years, our Dad fell ill and died shortly afterwards. All of us have tasted the pain of losing a loved one—and many more may. Dad's demise meant a bitter life experience for me. But since God knows best, we did not have to understand what He was up to by allowing our Dad to die so early. Yet we trusted Him. We trusted that He will never leave us nor abandon us—and He never did.

The best of it all is that, no matter what you have gone through, you can evolve again. I believe the marital or career mess in your life should not imply the end of you. You can rise from the ashes—as God has lifted me. God lifts from the dust to glory. We will all sing Hannah's song.

We can learn from one another's mistakes. In this book, I have uncovered the many mistakes I made that resulted in how my life turned out. I do not want upcoming generations, particularly those who will be privileged to know my story,

INTRODUCTION

to repeat the same mistakes.

I am not seeking pity by writing my story. By documenting the paths God has taken me through and where He has brought me, I want my readers to know that God is God and He can make all things beautiful. My desire is that the content of this book will give hope, uplift, encourage and prove that we serve a living God, who is not a man to lie. May you find inspiration, strength, courage, and humility to wait upon the Lord in your difficult moments.

CHAPTER 1

Why Label Me?

Born and raised on the premises of the 37 Military Hospital Barracks until my teen years, the 37 suburban area of Accra was a familiar neighborhood and territory for close to 18 years. More than a home, this vicinity was for me—and at least four of my younger siblings, an educational hub, a business enclave and a religious community.

My Dad, Mr. Raphael Zuruba, had moved to live here after a couple of years in Takoradi with family members who had migrated from Northern Ghana to live and work in the South. He had his early life in Duusi in Ghana's Upper East Region, where he was born. Just as today, youth from Northern Ghana migrated to Accra, Kumasi, Takoradi and other parts of Southern Ghana to strive for better life in those days. Around the age of 20, my Dad made his first major migrant trip to Kumasi in congruent with the trend at the time, but later moved to Takoradi where he had other relatives—uncles and aunties and many cousins. He transitioned from Takoradi to live at the 37 Military Hospital Barracks on the invitation of Sargent Yarog, his maternal uncle.

Mr. Yarog was a Staff Sergeant in the military. Not a high rank it was—and I remember he was predominantly in the kitchen side of the barracks. Sargent Yarog knew a Nursing Sister, Major Adama Hamidu, who needed a domestic staff. Nursing Sisters were part of noncombat military personnel. Although they receive the military training, their roles typically excluded national defense or other military operations. Nursing Sisters, in particular, work in the healthcare facilities of the military. Through the recommendation of Uncle Yarog, my Dad was hired by Major Adama Hamidu and hence had the privilege to occupy the Boys' Quarters of her bungalow.

Mom would share with me what great woman Major Adama Hamidu was. Kind, loving and God-fearing, she extended so much of the love of God to my father, and would maintain him until she retired from the military. As Sister Adama was leaving the barracks, Major Daniella Baah-Tetteh was coming to replace her in her role. Major Daniella Baah-Tetteh, who also lived at the barracks, was privy to my father's hardworking attribute, including his humility and cheerfulness. "Can I maintain your Raphael so that he will continue to live in the barracks and work with me?" Sister Mensah approached Major Adama Hamidu as the latter's retirement neared. And of course, when they retired, they would usually go to their own homes, sometimes in their remote villages, where they weren't going to bring a domestic staff because they wouldn't have that privilege of accommodating and paying one. The services that were rendered to her by my Dad were included in the military job package, all of which are withdrawn upon retirement. As one leaves, the next person that comes in would also have to enjoy the benefits, in this case, Major Daniella Baah-Tetteh. So Major Adama Hamidu let go my Daddy, Sister Daniella Baah-Tetteh became his second employer.

Sister Daniella Baah-Tetteh would be one most amazing person my family would ever encounter. A very kind, loving, and gracious woman of God, she would take my Mom as her own daughter, and my Dad as her own son. In fact, Sister Daniella was a spoiler, and I will tell you why.

I would be my mother's first born, and it was around the time of Dad's employment with Sister Baah-Tetteh that I would be born. Being a staff of the maternity ward, she actually delivered me on the day of Mom's delivery. She made everyone aware that it was her daughter delivering, so they took extra care of my mother. The spoiler she is, Sister Daniella provided everything my mother needed, including all the baby foods I fed on. My Sister Cynthia, alias "C" and Solomon, our third born were birthed under the umbrella of Sister Daniella.

Dad was a handyman—or a Jack of all trades—running everywhere all the time and hardly ever staying at home. In addition to various gigs he did for extra income, Dad worked as a civilian employee in the military, as a mechanic and as a domestic staff for Sister Mensah. He didn't have time for anything—relaxation or social life; all he did was work hard to support his family. To the best of his ability, he ensured that his family was comfortable, his kids well-fed, clothed, had the basic things they needed and were in school.

Mom would share with me how my Dad was very good at ironing. The Nursing Sisters admired how he ironed their white uniforms and particularly their special cap. He possessed a special skill for ironing that cap that it stood out whenever he did. So it became a thing that almost all the Nursing Sisters wanted to bring their cap to Mr. Zuruba to iron for them. And he was simply delighted to serve, even when it took the little time he would have had to rest.

But he struggled financially—both he and his dear wife—and his neighbours knew it. The barracks was built like an open "compound house." As such, there was little privacy; everybody knew everybody's business. They knew how poor my parents were. Our neighbours nicknamed my dad "poor man". He was always running around doing something—anything—for any small amount of extra money. For his struggle and hustles, they named him "poor man".

Then they nicknamed my mother "Kayayo". In Ghana, kayayo or kayayei (plural) refers to head pottering. Many Northern girls—and sometimes women, who migrate to urban centres, engage in kayayei. And my mother was always running back and forth like my father was, as she did her home and petty businesses. The female neighbours in the barracks started calling her Auntie Connie Kayayo. Thus they labelled my Dad and Mom.

They labelled my parents by their circumstances. It is a thing with people. They place labels on people according to their issues or conditions. It is human nature—however wrong it is. Even in the Bible, we find it many times. "Rahab the prostitute" (Joshua 6:25); "Simon the leper (Mark 14:3–9); "The woman with the issue of blood" (Mark 5:25–34); Zacchaeus the tax collector (Luke 19). Mind you, that was derogatory, too. Or at least a stigma. Tax collectors were seen as traitors because they were Jews working for the Romans who ruled or colonized the Jews.

People who nickname others do not always do so to insult or stigmatize their victims. In Bible times for instance, such labels were used to distinguish one person from another. There were many people who bore the name Judas, or Simon, or Joseph, or Mary. When names were so common, labels were used as a distinguishing feature. Sometimes, references were made to their fathers or even mothers. For example, ***"David the king begot Solomon by her who had been the wife of Uriah (Matthew 1:6, NKJV).***

Yet even when their labelling is not ill-intentioned, it still hurt the victims. It is never a pleasant thing to carry a label. Worse still, people don't usually use positive accomplishments to label others.

WHY LABEL ME?

Hardly would someone's positive deeds become their label. A few people carry good reputations, both in Bible days and in our times. We all know that sounds pleasant in our ears, but when your label creates a negative impression of you, a lot is at stake for you.

Your issue—struggle, pain, disadvantage—can become your individual name or identity. But glory be to God. Today, God has settled that kayayo. When the woman touched the hem of Jesus's garment, the bleeding ceased. My mother has touched God's garment. Now she lives a beautiful life. She's no more Auntie Connie Kayayo.

But it goes to tell you how people perceive you or your life. She's kayayo so they probably thought she was going to be kayayo forever. Why would you call somebody that? I remember vividly always hearing them call her that. As I grew older, I became angry when I heard that. So whenever they said it, I frowned. And they could tell that I wasn't pleased with their comments, but of course, as a child, what could I do about it? But I did not like it. I did not like it although I could not protest. Why label me? We are all human, so why label me? Whether poor or rich or kayayei or doctor. Whether achiever or temporary failure, extroverted or introverted, bossy or submissive, crazy or gentlemanly. Don't label me. Don't call me what I don't want to be called.

Labels are powerful. They can destroy your self-esteem and reputation by practically defining people's perception of you. You have to work to break the power of any labels placed on you. Labels can determine people's expectation of you. Anybody who knew my parents with those tags will definitely not hold them in high esteem. They will not accord them any respect, only look down on them. They would not recognize their talents and capabilities or appreciate their God-given gifts. It can even affect their own self-confidence. They may have accepted the labels and allowed it to limit them in life.

I don't know what labels have been placed upon you. But you have to rise up and break their hold upon your destiny. They may have labeled you poor, kayayei, lazy, untrustworthy, unfaithful, cheat, selfish, addict, ugly, fat, loser, not smart, short, skinny, useless, Black, mean, illiterate, or whatever. I just want you to know that you can overcome these labels and even undo them. Don't accept labels from people. Let your mind and spirit reject them. If they call you weak, tell yourself you are strong. If they call you stupid, tell yourself you are smart. If they call you illiterate, educate yourself. If they call you anything you cannot change, remind yourself of other qualities that God has given you. For instance, you may be short but fine looking or intelligent. We all definitely have something good in spite of our shortcomings or weaknesses or failures.

It is important to try to get to the bottom of some of the comments or labels we get from people. They can serve as genuine criticisms that if we heed, can go a long way to help us turn things around for ourselves. For instance, if people cannot trust you with their secrets and thus label you as such, you can consider their comments and work things out.

Labels should challenge us to work hard to change things. If they called you poor, find ways to break through and achieve financial freedom. It may be painful, but like someone said, "Grow through the pain."

Sometimes, you may never be able to undo the label for yourself. You just have to forgive and let go. But you can remove it for the generations after you. Dad and mom worked hard, and God was faithful to them. He has rewarded their children for their service to Him and to people.

Today, none of us their 5 children can be labelled poor or kayayei.

CHAPTER 2

Epitome of a Good Samaritan

Soon enough, the time came for Sister Daniella Baah-Tetteh to retire. She left to continue to serve humanity in various capacities, including as a pastor in her church, the Apostles' Revelation Society she had won my Dad into. She was replaced by Sister Helena Dogbatse, also a Major in rank. Major Helena Dogbatse was already living at the barracks. (It's a complex of the nursing sisters). My family was well-known to her, and she most probably admired my Dad's attitude to work.

As I indicated, everybody admired my father's hard work and dedication—his boss ladies and the other Sisters at the complex of Nursing Sisters. He would always lend these Sisters a helping hand—to cut their lawns, iron their clothes and caps or to voluntarily offer them some form of service. When he was done with his duties at Sister Daniella's and was going home, you would hear, "Oh Mr. Zuruba, would you mind helping me with ironing my cap?" Or, "Could you spare me a moment of your time to change my bulb?" These Nursing Sisters always had something for him to do. And because he was willing to always help, they all took a great liking of him. So when Sister Mensah was leaving, Sister Helena Dogbatse was ready to take on my father, and that is how she became my Dad's employer.

It usually took long for one person to leave for the next person to come. So Dad and Sister Helena Dogbatse worked for a really long time again, and I was in school during the whole time.

Sister Helena Dogbatse was nice, although somewhat tough and strict. But we were grateful that she employed my father and paid him duly. She also provided us with shelter—because when God would later call Dad to glory, she would allow us stay in the Quarters.

We are all different people. Sister Helena Dogbatse was different from Sister Daniella Baah-Tetteh, and indeed, different from Major Adama Hamidu, my father's first employer. But although a little bit tough and strong, my father never had any issues with her at all. My father would not have any issue even when he lived with the devil himself. He was that humble and did whatever was expected of him. He actually allowed himself to be overused.

Unlike Sister Daniella, Sister Helena Dogbatse wasn't all that there for us. When my Dad started working for Sister Daniella, she took notice of the disciplined nature of my father, coupled with his hardworking quality. She reasoned that being a young man who was just about starting a family, he would need a stable income to be a responsible man. She also reasoned that, at some point, she was going to retire, and my father's fate would be uncertain. She wanted to make sure then, that when she retired, my father would be well established. Thus, Sister Daniella enrolled my dad in a mechanical training institution. Concerned that the next person who may replace her after her service may not be understanding or considerate of the plight of the poor young man, she made it her goal to see my father well established before she retired. As my father worked with her—taking care of her home, he was learning auto mechanic work at a mechanic training school. He graduated and became a very good mechanic, and hence the go-to person for all the mechanical problems with the cars belonging the Nurses and Sisters.

So my father had a profession as a mechanic courtesy Sister Mensah, his second employer, and lived with her in the barracks, working for her as domestic staff. But that was not all.

When an opportunity came for recruitment into the military, Sister Daniella Baah-Tetteh recommended my father and he was taken. He wasn't a full military personnel; he was recruited as a civilian employee. His duty was to man the gate of the hospital. Unlike the full military personnel who wore the camouflage, these civilian employees had a brownish uniform, and worked with the regular officers. They were like military men but only trained in basic military drills to serve as security men alongside the military men. When we were kids, we called them "Soldier Saman" or "Soldier Brown Uniform".

Dad became our "Daddy Soldier Brown Uniform", working at night in his brown "soldier uniform". It became a sort of a part-time job for him, and afforded him some benefits such as free medical care at the Military Hospital, which went a long way to sustain and support his family. He did the house chores during the weekend at Sister Mensah's house, and on the nights that he was off from the "Soldier Brown Uniform" duties, he ended up doing other gigs. These gigs typically involved serving as security man at the houses of a few "big men" around Dzorwulu, who hired him when he was available.

Sister Daniella Baah-Tetteh's example is worthy of emulation. Here was a woman not related to my father but was so much interested in and concerned about the stability of his future and the welfare of his family, and went to great lengths to do something significant about it. Sister Daniella Baah-Tetteh was an epitome of the Good Samaritan, a real neighbour to my father and his family. According to Jesus' story of the Good Samaritan, no one should go through life without endeavouring to touch and impact another life in the smallest or most significant way. No one should concentrate on only themselves—their own life, family, children or business and ministry. Instead, we must go out of our way to pick an outcast, orphan or poor person and touch their life with the love of Christ. That is how to be the Good Samaritan who reached out to a man that had fallen victim to robbery.

There are always people around us like that victim of robbery, people who have fallen victim to poverty, sickness, unwanted children, rape, abuse, illiteracy, or even death like my mom and us, her children. The essence of this popular Bible story is for those who are capable to reach out to such persons. Jesus told that story because He wants people like these to be reached out to.

After my Dad had passed on, we went through a difficult time while living with Sister Helena Dogbatse. She was quiet well-to-do. For instance, she had all her children living in America, and sending her stuff every now and then. But she would never lend us support. I remember times I went to her, hoping that she would just give me some money for school. "Madam, I need some money to buy a book, please." "Oh Ama, I don't have money at the moment. When I get some, I will give you some to buy it. Tell your mom to try harder, OK?"

Sister Helena Dogbatse was simply not there for us when we desperately needed her help. But that is normal, because not everyone is meant to be a part of your story or testimony. Hers was to provide us with the shelter, which she did, and maintained it that way until her retirement.

Perhaps because she had known us from when we were little kids, she wasn't going to throw us out. She was considerate in that aspect. The accommodation was to be occupied by her domestic staff. All that we needed to do to sustain it was to ensure that her house was clean, and other housework was done. When Dad was not around to perform them, his friends and family members that lived around came in on the weekends and cleaned the Sister's house. Dad had his cousins and relatives and friends who were part of 441, a large Northern community just behind the Barracks and Mamobi suburbs. Dad had been of support to them in many ways, including using his privileges to help them access medical care at the 37 Military Hospital. They volunteered to support us secure the apartment by doing Dad's work. They did the work on the premises—like the weeding, and my mother did the inside work—cleaning of rooms and washrooms. Thus, we were able to maintain the accommodation for a long time.

As time went by, Sister Helena retired and left. Then came another young Lieutenant Colonel, Sister Annie Naa Lartey. She was rather very fierce and intolerant. Even Sister Helena was better! Her arrival marked the end of our stay in the Sisters' Quarters—whether we were prepared or not. She did not have any connection or relationship with my Dad or his family. When she arrived, my mom took me with her to welcome her, as well as explain our circumstances to her. She was point blank about not wanting anybody in her Boys' Quarters. She wanted us out, and her decision was not negotiable.

Because we had no place to go, my mother decided to plead with her. "Madam, look at me. I'm a woman like you. I have five kids. My husband has just died. I don't have anything. I can't even rent one room." "Oh, no. I have my own cleaners to do my job for me, I don't need anybody. My cleaner will need the place." I must say Sister Annie Lartey was very rude to us. She actually forced us out, and we ended up living on the corridors of our neighbours within the apartment that we had lived in. We made our home on the veranda of that apartment. Some good neighbours let us put our stuff in their kitchen, while we slept on the benches in front of the apartments. Before everybody else got up, we usually rose in the early mornings and took our shower, dressed up and quickly disperse—to work, school or just out to find a place to hang around until it was time to come to bed again.

We tried to win Sister Annie's heart. So there were weekends I went there to wash and clean for her, but she just wanted us vacate the apartment. I believe not everyone is meant to be a blessing to you. It is not because they are wicked. They are simply not part of your journey. They are not supposed to take any credit for anything that occurs in your life.

CHAPTER 3

Don't Squash My Dreams

Growing up, I was an exuberant and carefree child, with a big vision for myself. I wanted to be a medical doctor, and everyone knew it. I used to address myself by the title "Doctor." And before I could come to terms with the reality of the trajectory of my life, I fancied myself living this childhood dream.

In spite of all the hardships my responsibilities heaped on my young self, I was fun-loving, and full of joy. And just like my parents, particularly my Dad, I was on good terms with all of our neighbours, who knew about my passionate inclination for medical practice and my self-acclamation. When my father's friends came around our home, they would intimately ask of me, "Where's Doc?"

When our neighbours wanted to entertain themselves, they would call me and playfully ask, "Ama, what is your name?" Ironically, they call me by my name and ask me to introduce myself to them. I, on my part, would stop and confidently look them in the face, and declare my self-proclaimed identity.

"My name is Dr. Mary Ama Zuruba-Duke."

They would burst into a laud laugh, and I would speed out of their sight—or on a good day, I would be offered, in return for putting a laugh on their faces, a baksheesh I could buy candies with. And those were interesting days in my life. My surname is originally a compound name: Zuruba-Duke. But somehow, I never got to write it in full. While my siblings stuck to the compound name, I left out "Duke". But when I was telling my name, I often stated it in full.

Addressing my little self as "Dr." became a thing of a joke. Everybody just knew that that was my name. I didn't shy away from it whenever I was asked. But how that was going to be possible was something I never thought about. All I knew was that I wanted to be someone great; I wanted to impact lives. But how I was going to get there or how that was going to happen was one thing I never thought of.

In reality, if I was going to be a doctor at that time, I had to have to come from a relatively wealthy background because medical education is expensive in Ghana. With the kind of suffering it took for my parents to put food on the table, I should not be talking about such big dreams.

I was born and raised in a very poor home—until grace liberated me. By 1980, about three years after I was born on May 14, 1977, I had upgraded to big sister status with the coming of my younger sister, Cynthia, aka "C". Around that time too, I was enrolled for my Kindergarten education at Good Star Preparatory School, a private school located within the Airport Police Church, and would continue with my Primary education in the same school. During this period, the school underwent "rebranding" many times, but its location remained same. It did transform in different shapes, and with each transformation came a new name. At one point, classes 5 and 6 were held under the trees on the church premises. Students from the police barracks located meters away from the church would pass by calling us names—"Adua Ase School", or "Adua Ase Fuor" to wit, "School Under Trees" or "Those Under Trees". But it all came to pass after we transitioned to the Airport Police Junior Secondary School, to complete our basic education.

By the time I was old enough, my mother relied heavily on my able assistance in many respects. While mom was a petty trader, dad performed his many menial jobs—working as a civilian employee in the Military, stationed as a watchman in the night at the hospital gate or wherever he was assigned; working as a mechanic at Auto Parts Ltd., Industrial Area, during the day; and working as gateman or watchman for a few people on the days he was off. Indeed, finally, on weekends, he worked as a domestic staff for a Nursing Sister at the 37 Military Hospital, his duties basically including maintaining the house, i.e., keeping the compound, washing her car and ironing her clothes amongst others. As such, he was always on the go, never stopping!

During this period of my early education through to the primary and JSS, I supported my mom with her occupation and trade as well as with house chores. A petty trader, she sold everything and anything that was in season—oranges, maize, plantain. She run the business of roasting maize or plantain for sale inside the barracks.

By Primary 6, I had added hawking of doughnut—otherwise known as bofrot—and sweet bad, to my hustle. One of our female neighbours at the barracks made bofrot and sweet bad—she alternates between the two. I was one of many young girls who retailed them in the early mornings. When employees—who were usually our customers—settled at work, we retired. I would come back home and pay her for the quantity I had sold, and take my profits to keep for my mom. I would then get ready and go to school.

When I started JSS, my school ran shifts. We had a double track system where a student alternated between a morning or afternoon track. Whenever I was in the morning shift, school closed by noon. By the time I would get home, there was work waiting for me. For instance, I would come to meet oranges peeled and arranged on a tray, waiting for me to go and sell. The moment I drop my school bag and changed clothes, I set off to sell my oranges—whether I had had something to eat or not.

During an afternoon shift, both mom and I would rise early. While she went directly to the surrounding villages—Oyarifa, Dodowa where she could get the produce at wholesale prices, I would go to the Mallam-Atta Market to buy items such as coconut and charcoal that accompanied the sale of the maize. We would rush out of the house early in the morning, while my siblings were sleeping and get these items. The barracks was built like a compound house. There were many occupants in a single block. Whether or not you were home, therefore, it was possible to have somebody keep an eye on your children or take care of them on your behalf. Our neighbours knew that I would wake up and go to the market. So we left, knowing our back is covered.

On occasion when only mom went to the market to buy goods, she would leave home at around 5:00am. Being the oldest amongst 5 children, I took up the responsibility of taking care of my siblings while she was away. It was also my responsibility to set fire, and make ready before she brought the fresh corns or plantains. If there remained maize from the previous day, I start grilling them first. I would begin selling those ones before the fresh ones arrived. Normally, by the time she would come from the farm with her fresh produce, it would be around 11:30. As she takes over from me, I rush home and prepare for my afternoon session school. Before I leave for school, I would often check to see if some of the grilled maize or roasted plantain were ready—I grab a piece, and you would find me chewing on my way to school.

Such was life as I knew it. I was in that kind of struggle until by God's grace, other opportunities began to open up. But I did it without remorse; of course I didn't know any better. These are the parents I had; this was the upbringing I had; and this was the life I knew. As much as it was hard on me, I did it without complaining. What else could I have done? I supported my mother to the best of my ability, while my father also did his best. The little that we all made, we put together, and that was how the family got to get by.

But all of our little incomes put together, we didn't generate much. Not enough to ensure I could have medical education, if even I had the brains—and zeal, for it. But I nurtured the dream of becoming a doctor. How naïve I was! But it afforded me a sense of belief that there was a greater purpose for me in life, and I worried not about how I was going to get there.

Looking back today as I think about these things, I realize how this relates to our relationships with God. The Bible says, **"But now, this is what the Lord says—he who created you, Jacob, he who formed you, Israel: "Do not fear, for I have** *redeemed you; I have summoned you by name; you are mine" (Isaiah 43:1, NIV)." It is also written that God has good plans for us—to prosper us and give us an expected end (Jeremiah 29:11).*

Sometimes, we have to act like the little me—having more faith and less worry. I was not worried about the processes I would need to go through to reach my dreams and my expected end. It is enough for us to know and rest assured that God can fulfil His promises in our lives. He has said He is going to bring us to an expected end. With the mindset that He is able and faithful, when the winds blow, we do not let the rolling billows of the sea cause our faith to move or get us worried. Instead, we have to have the faith that whatever it is, after every turbulence, the Father is going to take us to the expected end.

Before you can walk with God for a long time and have a good relationship with Him, you have to be like the child I was: an infant, who is naïve, and so not bothered about the cares of life, the details and nitty-gritties of the issues of life in order to be asking questions out of doubt.

Many times, we worry too much, and worry will not get us to our destination. Trusting God will. You may begin badly, but you can end well. Humble beginnings can still result in a great future. You may not know where the life is heading, but God has the master plan; and His plans for us are good as the Scripture says.

In spite of all my struggles, I performed well in my BECE, and I was admitted into a Senior Secondary School (SSS), Krobo Girls' Secondary School.

CHAPTER 4

Should You Really Quit?

As the blazing afternoon sun quickly died down, rays of the setting sun began to cast slanting strikes across the buildings on the premises of the 37 Military Hospital Barracks, and on vehicles and people journeying towards their abode after the day's activities, using the route in front of the Hospital Nursing School Hostel, where Mom's business was located. Here, she roasted maize—and sometimes plantain or cocoyam and yam for sale to her customers, who were predominantly the many Nursing Students and 37 Military Hospital primary school pupils who used that route.

Her able assistant, when I was not in school, I was always present by her side, aiding in all aspects of the activities that went into this petty trade—peeling and roasting, poking fire, carefully wrapping and packing for buyers and receiving monies and giving out changes.

Around evenings like this when we prepared to round up our day's commercial activities, expectation of Dad was high, as he usually made it back home around this time, riding his bicycle. An employee of Auto Parts Ltd., one of Accra's biggest automobile dealerships, he saved on his income by avoiding boarding vehicle to and fro work. His age-old bicycle was his means of transport to work each morning and back home at the end of each day's labour—a total of about 8 kilometers.

Each time he came home, Dad brought candies to all of us the neighbourhood kids. The candy companies had a sense of humor. Or maybe they wanted to appeal to kids. They often molded their products into funny shapes—handbags, shoes, glasses and stuff like that. Dad usually got them from his workplace around the Industrial Area. If it was not candy, it was always something else, such as someone always getting a ride on his bicycle. We loved it very much, hence, looking forward to his coming became a ritual.

"Dad is coming!" I announced when I spotted my father riding his bicycle up the street from the

entrance of the Nursing Sisters' Quarters towards us. I noticed he had a load strapped to his bicycle. I figured it was my mattress I was to take to the boarding house. With an unusual excitement on his face, he proudly rode up the road. I left my mom's side at the sight of him.
Running as fast as I could, I met him just meters away, surrounded by my childhood mates. My mattress. I couldn't contain my joy. My dream of going to the Secondary School was closer than I had imagined.

Dad had ridden his bike with my mattress all the way from Industrial Area, behind Circle, where he worked and where the mattress dealer— Memory Foam—was located. Of course, there were outlets closer to our home than that, but there, he must have gotten it at the wholesale price. And rode it to our home at the barracks. He was obviously very proudly excited to have purchased her daughter's mattress.

Gaining admission into Krobo Girls' Secondary School came as joy news to myself and family. It was my parents' desire to see their children climb up high on the academic ladder, and I was setting the pace. Yet at the same time, making that dream a reality became a very big challenge for my poor parents as Secondary School cost so much at the time. Though my father didn't have the money, he didn't want the opportunity to slip by. Indeed, he was really poor; he didn't have a car, he didn't have any properties or any such thing, yet he determined to put me through school. As the days went by, he and my mom gathered the items on my prospectus—from trunk to bucket and plates and clothes until all was set, and the date came for me to go to school.

Much as my father would have wished to go with me to school, he had to relinquish the role to his brother, Mr. Ayaba, (also of blessed memories) as he was not educated enough to handle the paper works to be carried out by wards on arrival. And they both couldn't afford to go with me.

I settled in school, poised to excel above my peers in the Science class. Quite luckily, my parents ensured I was somewhat comfortable. Although they did not have money, they tried to make sure I didn't lack too much. They provided enough to keep me at school. I never ran out of provisions—gari, milk power, milo, shitor. Dad did his best to get my textbooks—although sometimes, he could only afford a few of out the total number. I remember the first biology textbook he got me—it got me so happy. I carried it to class with pride to the full view of my mates—just like almost everyone else who had one did. In my mind, I knew I was on my way to becoming a doctor. I appreciated the efforts of my parents. As little as what they could get me were, I was always content, and never envied what my friends had. By God's grace also, I had good friends who supported me as often as possible. When I didn't have, God aligned people that would provide for me. For instance, I had school mothers that were so kind to me. Also, when school fees payments were due, I didn't know how my dad and mom managed to raise the monies, but my fees were often paid.

However difficult life was for my parents and us their children, we made progress as the days went by. Challenges shouldn't stop us. Problems, afflictions, suffering, persecutions, labels—whether true or not, should not be able to hinder our progress. We should be able to advance in spite of all the limitations we face. Difficulty is not impossibility. "It is difficult" does not mean "It is impossible." Life is both hard and beautiful. Happiness and sadness and joy and hurt are all aspects of it. But we can progress in spite of anything.

You are an Israelite walking in the wilderness towards your Promised Land. You are in the wilderness now, but you are making progress towards your home on the Promised Land. As day and night appears and disappears, you are advancing in age and in achieving your goals. You are advancing academically, financially, socially, spiritually. Before you know it, you are living the dream, if you do not quit.

My family was in continual crisis. For a long time, we were unable to make ends meet. I started school doubling as a part-time labourer. But gradually, I moved from the Baby Schools to Primary, went on to complete Junior Secondary and passed excellently, and enrolled at the Senior Secondary level. In the midst of the challenges, I was making progress. Against the odds, I was making progress.

You can make progress, too. Gradually, you can get somewhere. Gradually, you could be getting closer and closer to your dream or goals. Gradually, you could be getting closer to your purpose, your promise, your prophecy, your destination, your Promised Land. Should you really quit just because it is difficult? Just because you have come face-to-face with the Red Sea? Just because you have to forfeit meat and eat only manna for a season? Just because of a temporal dry season of no water? Should you really return to Egypt, the land of slavery just because of a few challenges? Should you really quit when it is only difficult but not impossible?

Should you really quit when there is light at the end of the tunnel? When after a temporary failure, you could make a lasting success? When you know instant success is only a myth? When you really need to succeed? When the world is waiting to celebrate you? When you know nothing good comes easy? When your past failures cannot determine your future successes? When being still alive means hope? When, deep down, you believe you can and have the faith to succeed? When you would surely regret the chances you don't take? When you are destined to succeed anyway? When you are so talented and gifted for it? When not succeeding is dangerous to your survival? When the younger and future generations are looking up to you? When it can only get better in the coming days?—should you really quit?

Should you really quit and give up when the Bible says you must run to win (1 Corinthians 9:24); when the Bible says you must not get weary because you will reap in due season (Galatians 6:9)? Should you really quit?

CHAPTER 5

A Great Heavenly Reward

Two years had passed swiftly since I enrolled at the Krobo Girls' Secondary School. The long vacation soon ended, too, and school had just reopened. I was about entering the third and final year.

Reopening date was 13th September, 1993. I was ready to leave home for school, and as usual, my dad sat me down to have a conversation with me, and rehearsing to me some of his favorite lines. "I was not fortunate to receive education. But I am trying my best to ensure that you attain it to the highest level. I will continue to work hard for you. Your part is to study hard. Study very hard, Ama! Make your books your best friend."

I listened actively and nodded my head many times.

"Always believe that God is the foundation of everything you intend to do! So you have to be prayerful," he added.

Finally he said, "Remember the home you are coming from and be satisfied with the little that you have. Is that okay?

"Have you packed all your things?"

"Yes, Dada."

"Good. Do have a safe journey. Goodbye!"

"Thank you very much, Dada. Goodbye."

At that, father and daughter parted ways, hoping to meet again during Christmas holidays, about 13 or so weeks away. He left for work, and I finished up later and set off, too. As I walked pass the emergency ward of the hospital towards the station to pick car to school, I saw my dad on his way back—to my surprise as I wasn't expecting him.

He met me and said, "Ama, I want to come and say goodbye to you again, and be sure you have secured transportation and are on your way before I go to work." I was surprised because he had never done a thing like that before. He took my hand, and with my bag on my back, we walked towards the lorry station.

"Dada, I want one of these sandals," I requested of him, pointing to a new brand of sandals that was in vogue then, popularly called Okpanka sandals. It was a brown sandals that many students had. "Everyone in my school got one, except me," I said, obviously exaggerating. "So please, when we vacate, I want one for the next term," I added. Dad agreed to get me one, and we went into the station.

Only seven days later, my school's headmistress invited me to her home one afternoon. She detained me for the rest of the day, and even made me have dinner with her before releasing me to return to the dormitory. I knew Mrs. Agnes Akoto did like me, but not to the extent of giving me such nice treatments. No matter how much a tutor was pleased with a student, expressing it did not include sharing their home and dining table. If the headmistress was doing this for any reason, I could hardly place a finger on it.

The next day, I was informed that I had a visitor—during non-visiting hours. It was one of our neighbours, Mr. Dadibo. We had developed such great family friendship with Mr. Dadibo that we now call him Uncle. "Daddy has asked me to bring you home, Ama. There's a festival we're celebrating. It would be good for you to see it," he said. Excited, I went back to the dormitory and packed a few things and left with him.

As we approached home, he left me to go into the house alone because he wanted to collect an item from a friend down our block. As I approached further, some of our neighbours kept coming out from their blocks. I think I overheard one of them speak aloud and said, "Ama is coming" and the rest of them began to mutter under their breath.
I entered the house and met people sitting all over, and on the corridor. Unaware what was going on, I started greeting everyone, "Good afternoon."

"How are you, Ama?" they would ask, and break down weeping. I was growing suspicious, but managed to keep my cool, responding, "I'm fine, thank you." It was a festival I was invited to by my father. I was going in to see him. If anything had happened, at least, I would know the moment I see my Dad.

I went past everyone and entered the living room. What greeted my eyes was my mom lying on the floor and rolling from one end to the other. At that moment, my countenance chanced. I immediately knew something was wrong. It must be my father! "What has happened to my

A GREAT HEAVENLY REWARD

father?" I asked. Everybody burst out crying.

I don't remember what happened next. I must have blacked out. But when I got back to my senses, I thought very deeply, asking myself so many questions. What's going to become of you, Ama, now that the breadwinner of our family is gone? It dawned on me. "This is the end of me." How do I move on without my father? Even when he was there, we struggled. How much more now? Now that my mom had become a single mother of five young children; and I, a half orphan with four younger siblings. I knew the consequences of all this—the struggle my mom was going to go through to raise the five of us. But—well, it had happened already; what could I do?

In all my wildest imaginations, I could never believe that when Dad returned to say goodbye that September 13th when I was leaving for school, it was the last I would see him. When our neighbours saw me approach and muttered under their breath, I still had no clue they were wondering what my reactions were going to be, knowing how close I was with my father, and how deadly his sudden death would hit me.

Little did I know that Mr. Dadibo abandoned me to go into the house alone because he could not stand the sight of me receiving the devastating news of my father's demise. Unknown to me, he had come to my school the day before to inform the school authorities about my father's demise, and sought permission to take me home with him the next day. He had left to spend the night at his hometown of Dodowa, located close to my school.

Now also, it made so much sense why Mrs. Akoto pampered me the way she did that day. But of all the reasons that came to mind to justify her actions, death was not one of them. Who would have assumed that all the nice treatments were to compensate for, and to console me, for the loss of my dear father?

Dad had taken ill a week after seeing me off to school. On the morning of September 19th, the day before he would die, he was seen working laboriously at Sister Helena's house. He tidied up the entire compound and put the house in order. One of the female servants in the Nursing Sister's house related that He had come to her asking for anything that needed fixing so he could "do it at once."

A GREAT HEAVENLY REWARD

"Mr. Zuruba, Are you going somewhere? Why are you working so extremely hard today?" the female servant queried.

"Let me just fix them, my sister, since I have the time. I'm not sure when I'm coming back to do it." But little did she know that he was speaking in parables.

As he finished with the work in the house, he went to work on a coconut tree on the compound. "This coconut is ripe; let me harvest it," he was heard saying. That same day, he decided to prune an old palm tree on the premises—"to see if it will bear again." A neighbour met him and said, "Mr. Zuruba, you've spent a long time here today."

"Yes, Auntie, I want to finish everything and be relieved," he responded heartily. But nobody ever thought or assumed that death was beckoning.

When he got home, he continued to work, cleaning and placing things in order in our home. "Let, me just clean here too, Comfort," he said to his wife who was wondering what had gingered him to go the extra mile that day.

A short while later, he complained of not feeling well. He started developing headache. When his condition did not improved by the next day, our Mom walked him to the hospital to seek medical care. They were told he would have to be admitted. It was quite a surprise because he walked into the hospital by himself, which meant he shouldn't be so sick that he had to be admitted. They did not take anything with them, as they were not expecting to be admitted. My mom left to come and get a few things they would need while on admission. But upon return to the hospital, she was told her husband had died!

It was a big shock to everybody—particularly those who had seen him working the day before in the open premises of the hospital barracks. My Dad was one most hardworking man. He laboured all his life. But he never enjoyed the fruits of his labour. Today, as I write, I had made it big. His vision for me—and indeed, for us his children, has come to pass. If he were alive today, he would be reaping the fruits of his hard labour. We could come together and clothe, feed and shelter him to give him a comfortable life. But unfortunately, he went to be with the Lord much earlier.

Life is sometimes like that. Like my dad, there are people who work really hard, bless people, serve God well, but who do not get to reap the fruits of their labour here on earth. It must be painful for them, and especially for their living relatives who sit at table, shop brand new clothes, sleep on cozy beds, all alone, because those they hold dear are not around to share in their blessing.

My consolation is in knowing that heaven is a far better place to be. It doesn't matter if we don't reap our rewards on earth. What is more important is making it to heaven and enjoying eternal rewards. My Dad did not live long to enjoy the blessings that God has bestowed on me and my siblings today, but I know he is happier in heaven.

Our rewards—the best of them—are with God in heaven. In heaven, we have eternal life. A life of peace with God. A life of eternal joy. We are assured in the Bible Book of Revelations, ***"And God will wipe away every tear from their eyes; there shall be no more death, nor sorrow, nor crying. There shall be no more pain, for the former things have passed away" (Revelations 21:4, NKJV).*** If there is any goal to pursue on earth above all else, it must be the goal of going to be with the Father one day.

The sad thing is that there are people whose pursuit are only earthly. They make no effort to work out their salvation, and their place in the life hereafter. Jesus said, ***"But lay up for yourselves treasures in heaven, where neither moth nor rust destroys and where thieves do not break in and steal" (Matthew 6:20, ESV).*** Worst of all are those who do not even believe that there is a God, and who will judge all peoples on a Judgment Day.

My biggest advice to us is, whatever we do, we have to ensure that we are working for the life hereafter. This world is not our home. We are transitioning through it into eternity. It takes a relationship with Jesus to have peace in eternity. And I invite you to accept Him into your life today.

CHAPTER 6

Angels in Human Form

In the days that followed, arrangements were made, and Dad's funeral rites took place. Sympathizers poured out in their numbers, with many of them, especially, Dad's friends and relatives, promising us their support. In the aftermath of it all, everyone left—just as they had come. They left, leaving my Mom and my siblings alone.

It seems to me that, in life, you have lovers only when you are alive. Relatives and friends demonstrate love to you as long as you have breath. If death takes you away, it takes your memory with it. If you do not prepare well, your family will be plunged into instability and crisis. As much as my father did not have anything, he was a kind and loving man. His friends and siblings sought counsel from him often. They travelled far and wide to Mr. Zuruba for words of wisdom and encouragement, and he was always there for them in that respect. He was not educated, but he supported his siblings when they had the opportunity to go to school. He worked and supported them the best he could before he got married. By the time he died, they were well-established and settled—in Takoradi and elsewhere. Aware of this, we thought we had family, who would reach out and help us. I was even expecting that some of them would come and adopt us to live with them so that they take care of us till we complete our second cycle education. But I was greatly mistaken. My father's family completely abandoned us to our fate.

When I was due going back to school, I didn't have to worry about my term's fees, because they had been paid by Dad. But right after vacation, I started having problems paying my fees promptly, because my mother couldn't raise them.

I remember on one of those occasions, she travelled all the way to one of our uncles at Takoradi to solicit his support. She explained to him that she did make some money from her trading activities, but it could only suffice to cater for feeding and other housekeeping expenses. It wasn't sufficient to cover capital expenses like our education and rent. Instead of helping my mother with some money, my Uncle advised her to give me out to be married. In his opinion, since I, her oldest daughter, have had some level of education—up to form three, it was sufficient. I have had enough schooling. At that stage and age, I was ripe for marriage. He suggested that marrying me off would be a profitable venture. The prospective suitor would be required to pay, as our custom as Northerners demands, four cows as dowry. The worth of the cows could be accepted in cash. According to my Uncle, we could count on that money to take care of my remaining siblings.

When my uncle told that to my mother, she came back to Accra in tears, having spent the little she had to board car to and from Takoradi. His advice didn't sit well with her, so she rejected it, and vowed to take care of her children by the sweat of her brows. She had the faith that the God who called her husband would not let her and her children face disgraced.

We had to continue to hustle our way through, working menial jobs and trades to support ourselves in any way we could. I thought I had seen hardship growing up. But this was even worse. It was challenging on every side.

In the final year, I was required to register for SSSCE, the final examination. My Mom could not afford it. It took the intervention of a church, the International Central Gospel Church (ICGC), to take care of my fees. One couple who lived with us at the barracks, Mr. and Mrs. Amuzu, drew close to me and kept an eye on me when my dad died. During my bereavement, they used to come for me to their house. They opened me up to the Word of God in those broken moments of my life, and prayed with me. Indeed, I became like an adopted child to this couple, and they were there for me. Being members of the ICGC, they used to go with me to their services and prayer meetings, as well as their dawn prayers and cell meetings long before the passing on of my father.

They didn't have money, too, but when my Mom told them she wasn't able to raise money to register me for the final exams, they went to inform the cell group, and the elders made contributions for us. They later relayed the matter to the church and the church responded by paying for the rest of my school fees and registration for my final exams. God used Mr. and Mrs. Amuzu to help me get the help I needed to register and write my

ANGELS IN HUMAN FORM

final exams—and I did well.

Mr. & Mrs. Amuzu—and the ICGC were, to me, angels in human form, and if all of us tried to be like them, the world would be a paradise. To those who find themselves in circumstances as mine, be on the lookout for angels in human form. God always sends them. Pray and ask Him to send yours if they haven't come to you.

Although I passed all my subjects and desired strongly to advance my education, I had no hope of furthering. I had to stop and work to support my siblings. After graduating from the SSS, I had plenty of time to help my Mom roast her corn and plantains at her usual spot. Hawking now prohibited in Accra, I had to stop going to sell at the roadside, in order to not risk getting my goods seized and being beaten by military police deployed against offenders.

But now a graduate of the SSS, my mind was a little developed. I could find other jobs, and be in a better position to support my Mom to raise my siblings. Around that time, a friend found a job advertisement in a newspaper. A popular private lotto operator, Asare Original Pay All, was hiring female checkers. I rushed quickly to apply and I was hired! Coming in as a checker, I was one of many girls employed to go through the lotto books to pick out the winning ones. I was just excited to have my first real job—indeed, my breakthrough moment it was!

Not long after that we received my father's little pension money. With that money, we rented a chamber and hall at Madina Zongo, and moved out of the 37 vicinity. It was somewhat an upgrade—from a single room Boys' Quarters, where we had spent our life until now, to our first chamber and hall apartment. We also got our first hunchback TV!

At some point before we would leave 37, mom got a cleaning job at the State House through one of my father's family members who was in charge of hiring the cleaners! So from the time we moved to live at Madina, Mom did not trade again. She traveled to State House every day, whiles I went to Lapaz! Mom continued to work in State House until she retired officially in 2021. (She took an early retirement to move to the States in 2018 and officially retired in 2021).

I started to save up money from my checker job at Original Pay All. In spite of all the difficult things that we went through as a family, I look back and appreciate every trajectory that my life took.

ANGELS IN HUMAN FORM

The trajectory of my life has been complicated, misunderstood, misdiagnosed, but I appreciate all my flaws and experiences. I am not ashamed to speak about them on any platform. They are what have shaped me to become who I am today. These past experiences are helping me to relate to the younger generations. The Lord Himself must have allowed things to go that way. God allows us go through many things because He has to use them in preparing us. You will need all of the experiences that you acquire going through those things.

I believe God could have easily brought somebody my way to help me when I was struggling. My father's siblings were not that broke. They were relatively well-to-do. It amazes me that my Dad is singled out as the poor one among them. They were well-to-do enough to have offered us food and clothing and shelter, but they did not. But you don't have to worry when people you think should help you refuse. They are not part of the plan of God for you. Sometimes, for the glory of God to manifest, you will suffer. You will go through things—fall, suffer, fail, be rejected.

Today, I hold no grudges against anyone. I love my uncles and my other family members. I have come to realize that those who withheld help from us when we needed it were not chosen by God to provide for us. It is the reason why God hardened their hearts. He made their hearts like Pharaoh so that His glory will manifest in our lives. He wants that through my testimony, He will lift someone. A widow without hope—without food to eat or shelter. But when she hears about us, she should be able to say, "If God could plant Comfort and her children where they are today, then I can have hope in God, too."

A teenager hawking fruits on the streets or retailing corn or plantain by the wayside, hungry and poor, and begging alms, has today become someone in life. When once upon a time, her family didn't have a name, yet this girl wasn't afraid to dream big, and hope that someday, a bright future could be hers—a future of hope. I went through it all so that today, I could encourage someone.

CHAPTER 7

Don't be Quick to Judge Me

A little grown up this time also, I began to look beautiful and attractive. Men started expressing interest in me. Not long after joining Asare Original Pay All, one of their managers approached me one day and said he loved me. He looked like a nice man, but my preoccupation at that point in my life was every support that would ease the burden on me, as I was still on the hustling journey, trying to make ends meet, trying to support my family. As a young girl going through so much, financial relief was all that mattered to me. Being a manger and thus a bigger earner, I assumed he could be of immense "benefit" to me. Thus, I accepted to go out with him.

Giving in to the proposal of Kofi—as would come to fondly call him—was not an acceptance to marry him. I was far from the stage where I would make a decision about settling down. But accepting him into my life would mark the beginning of a long journey that God was going to take me on. A journey on which He would allow me make many mistakes, but more importantly, a journey that will birth my purpose in life.

At only 19 years old, I was pretty young when Kofi and I met. Being in his thirties, he was much older than me. He knew just how to spoil me and make me feel loved. He bought my first birthday champagne when I turned 20, and the celebration remained a milestone event for me. Besides being young, Kofi noticed I was smart and determined, and thought I still should further my education. With his support and encouragement, I started secretarial training at Dadd Secretarial School, alongside working.

Kofi had his good sides which drove me to love with him very much, but he had an "adventurous" side that drove him to engage in relationships with several other women. I didn't like that about him, but being the very quiet, shy, humble and respectful type—as well as much, much younger, I was so naïve he played on my intelligence.

DON'T BE QUICK TO JUDGE ME

I have regret many times all that had gone on between Kofi and me, and wondered why on earth I couldn't foresee it all coming. Why didn't I heed the warnings—from my mom and his colleague workers who told me things?

But as I advanced in my studies, I would realize that I found security in being in his arms as the older person he was. It was out of my trauma and fear of being rejected and abandoned I clung to him. I desired a fatherly or male figure in my life, owing to the vacuum created by my father's demise. Indeed, our third sibling was our only brother and male figure in our lives. He was himself a kid when our father passed on. So we had no male figure to "protect," discipline, straighten, and provide for us. So when I met this guy that showed me he loved me, cared about me, and was willing to help me, I clung to him. I was afraid of losing him, not for who he was, but for what I was receiving from him. It was why I held tightly on to him in spite of everything. I did, although I did not fully understand the relationship—or what I was really doing.

In spite of his claims to love me seriously, I saw and heard too many bad things about him and other women that was sufficient to make me desist from having anything to do with him.

Only God knows what made me stay.

Not that I did not feel hurt and complain. His lifestyle resulted in frequent breakups characterizing our relationship, and a sense of insecurity at both ends would cause a lot of issues when I would leave the company for an opportunity elsewhere. I was offered an internship by Lever Brothers, now Unilever Ghana Limited, and at that point, I quit my job at Asare Original Pay All.

At Unilever Ghana Limited, I met one of our biggest suppliers, another Kofi, who admired me and wanted to date me. Before I could decide whether it was time to call it quits permanently with Kofi and move on, I heard that he was seeing another lady, although he would deny it when I confront him. I knew who he was, so I didn't need to believe him. I decided it was payback time for him. He ought to experience how it felt to have your love taken from you. I started dating my new Mr. Kofi. As a young girl, my focus remained acquiring resources to support my family and not the hurt I was inflicting on others. As much as I was aware, I knew it was for a moment. Having broken up with Kofi, I wanted to live a rich life to prove myself.

But my old Kofi would not give up on me. He kept chasing me whiles I was with my new Kofi. He never stopped. No, not for a minute! Of course I knew I still loved him, but at that material time, I was comfortable and gaining a taste of richness my new Kofi lavished on me. As old Kofi persisted, I reached an agreement with him to continue to see him, too. The idea to travel out of the country came up. My old Kofi's friend's girlfriend was into a travel and tours business. We agreed that I would make efforts to get money from my rich lover for us both to leave the country. It sounded pretty nice to me, and I started putting the plan into action.

It was the most complicated part of my life. But I am sure onlookers misunderstood me. They would not consider that I was going through challenging circumstances, except to judge me. "She's seeing someone's husband." No one ever stopped to think or ask what had driven me—a fine descent girl into that condition. "This is not the Ama we knew. Ama used to be a very good girl growing up. But now she has become a different person; what has happened? What can we do to help her situation?" No one ever thought to ask. It is for this reason I can never forget Mr. and Mrs. Amuzu. They didn't criticize. They reached out instead. They understood my circumstances—and did something about it.

Many people are quick to judge. They are keen about judging, condemning and lashing out at people when they err. It appears that many people in our societies are on the constant lookout for faults in other people so that they can judge and condemn them. It seems that in their hearts, people are secretly wishing that other people will falter in life so that they can find a reason criticize, judge and condemn them.

How sad! They are not concerned about or interested in understanding the factors that push people into doing the wrongs they criticize. They are not interested in offering a helping hand to lift them out of their circumstances. They are more interested in condemning than seeing people come out of those conditions for which they are judging them.

They are excited about creating a long list of blacklisted individuals who become their topic for gossip than being concerned for how they could be transformed into glory. They can't seem to wait to see them face the consequences of their actions. They somehow love to see them repaid for their iniquities than to see them repent and consequently escape the consequences of their actions. People engaging in vices most like end up paying dearly for their actions, but that is what some people seem to wish for others.

It is a common thing for people be critical. But I want to advise you against it. Do not be quick to judge others. Every cause has an effect, and every effect has a cause, we know. Very often, you are going to find people living a life that does not befit our faith, or walking in ways not worthy of our calling. Don't sit somewhere and pass judgments about them. You don't know their struggles. You don't know what difficulty they are going through. You don't know why they have to act or behave that way.

When you see people engaging in what is unbecoming of a Believer, or what falls below our society's standards, stop and ask yourself, "What can I do about this? How can I help him or her become a better person—the kind of person I won't judge? How can I reach out and perhaps caution this person?

After going through all that I have been through—the lows and highs, this is the kind of person I have become. This is the mindset I have developed out of my experiences. To reach out when I notice people in certain conditions or lifestyles that is being criticized by others. I have learned to see beyond what a person does to what accounts for their behaving that way. Perhaps because of my background, but I am able to put myself in others' shoes, and ask, Why does that child have to do this? What is the reason behind this behaviour? What is the root cause of their actions? What can I do? Can I step into the shoes of Mr. and Mrs. Amuzu and do what they did for someone today?

I thank God that every good thing they deposited in me during the time I was learning under their feet did not go waste. My poor mother was disappointed and heart-broken during this phase of her daughter's life. Of course, my old Kofi's family adored me and wanted me in their family. But my Mom tried many times to talk me out of it; I was reluctant to change my mind. In spite of her fierce objections, Kofi and I kept it going little by little, and everyone knew we had something going at the same time that I had others like my new Mr. Kofi in my life. She, like many others, feared I was on the path to destruction, but God was at work. Indeed, I was headed for pain and hurt, but God would turn my ashes into beauty.

CHAPTER 8

Dear Wayward Teen's Parent

I hated Sundays growing up. The idea of Sundays just sickened me. Those family Sabbaths were a hell of a time for me and my siblings. Although I never really had a favourite day because every day of my childhood was a pain day, Sundays were worse. They were never welcomed. For many reasons, Sundays weren't days I looked forward to. No, I didn't have to hawk on Sundays. It was a taboo for members of Daddy's church, the Apostles' Revelation Society he was introduced to by Major Daniella Baah-Tetteh, to buy or sell on Sundays. Rather, my dislike for Sundays was born out of the laborious efforts that went into church attendance. Sundays were notorious for long distance treks—to and from church, usually in the hot sun, and most certainly on empty stomachs.

Growing up with my father, we never took churching for granted. From where we lived at the 37 Hospital Barracks, the entire family went on foot from home to my father's church at Pig Farm, the next suburb. We didn't have a car and we didn't have money for transportation, except for some occasions when dad would walk and we kids and mom would take trotro (public transportation). We often couldn't afford to pay for every one of us, so my sister 'C' would sit on my laps and my other siblings on mom's laps. Sometimes, some kind passengers would offer to help mom carry my siblings on their laps. Other than that, walking was mostly the only option most of the time. Except for long intercity travels or journeys, boarding vehicles wasn't a regular part of our family culture. Dad himself used a bicycle for nearly all his rounds. But he could not rely on it to transport his entire family to church. Missing church was out of the question, and unavailability of a means of transportation was no excuse. So on most Sundays, rain or shine, we walked to church in and out on foot.

I never liked it, and I am sure you wouldn't either, if you were in my shoes. Those long treks seemed as severe punishments. It was just the next suburb, but to my little feet, the distance seemed endless. Lack of money can make a parent seem wicked. As hungry as I would be after the forenoon service, Daddy wouldn't even pamper me with an ice-cream or a drink. I watched, envious, as parents who could afford to, bought yoghurt or drinks and pastries for their kids. The whole experience made me just abhor Sundays. I could get so angry just because it was a Sunday.

But, looking back today, I acknowledge that those were not wasted efforts. It was a good seed that Daddy was sewing in us, and by the time he died, this seed was ready to germinate, grow up and bear fruit. Even though at a point, we were not living by the Word of God and the principles we had learnt from church, the seed had been planted and was growing.

My father himself a very God-fearing man, and having raised us in the fear of God, my going wayward in my late teens took many people by surprise. The fear of God my father had instilled in me apart, I also used to be a very shy kid growing up. I was just a good kid—humble and respectful. But a couple of years after losing my dad, things began to change. I had to bear a lot of responsibilities—including supporting my siblings through school. As a result of the financial pressure those responsibilities placed on me, I accepted proposals from men on the basis of their financial statuses. During the short period between 16 and 17 years, I had begun to follow my own inclinations and lapsed into waywardness.

As much as I believe my going through those experiences were inevitable, there was no way I could remain wayward after having been brought up the way my parents did. I was supposed to go through those stages. They are stages of life no one can run away from. They are moments during which every young person would need someone to take hold of them and redirect their path, or they could be completely lost.

But my father had prepared us beforehand for moments like that. He had sown in us the seed of the fear of God. Although illiterate, he bought me my own Bible. During Bible Studies at church, I was required to note down every quotation referenced in the studies. I would later read them with him when we got home. He was pretty busy—the only day he was home and a full time Daddy was Sundays, and he spent it judiciously with us.

Dad was not controlling when it came to where I wanted to worship, as long as I was in a Bible-believing church. He permitted our neighbors and surrounding churches to help me grow in the Lord. I would go to week day services at the 37 Military Hospital Presbyterian and Methodist Church, and sometimes the Church of Pentecost. These gave me a strong foundation in the Christian Faith. As such Daddy's seed he sowed in me was watered by diverse sources. Indeed, before his demise, I had stopped going to his church and become more grounded in the ICGC. As a member of the ICGC, I was also in the cell meeting hosted by Mr. and Mrs. Amuzu.

Dad thus raised us in the way we should go that we would not depart from when we were old (Proverbs 22:6). That is why I think the example of my father is worthy of emulation by all parents. I should urge all parents to plant this same good seed in their children. When you raise them in the fear of the Lord from their childhood, even when they begin to go wayward in their adolescence, you can rest assured that they will return home like the prodigal son. You can only have cause to worry or be afraid when you have not planted a good seed in them.

All teenagers go through these stages where they think they should be given liberty to do what they please. When they come into their primetime—in the full glory of their beauty—their hips and breasts and other body contours glaring, they assume they have arrived. But let them do all they please, life experiences will humble them and they will come back home to order—once you have planted that seed in them. In the midst of it all, the seed in them will be fighting for space in their inner self, until it overpowers all the other forces.

Don't panic, or be worried about the shame or embarrassment they may bring you when they backslide. Don't judge them either. Don't give up on them. God is at work in their lives. He is ordering their steps and it will go well with them. What God needs you to do is partner Him to work in their lives and get them to where He is taking them.

More importantly, this is not the time to curse or reject them. All they need is your intercession. It is what my mom did. Today, I am a blessing to her. Today, I am a child she is proud of. The future she desired for is what I have attained, though not through the processes she would have wished. But indeed, the most important thing is that I did not remain lost. I found my way back to God, and to His purpose for me.

DEAR WAYWARD TEEN'S PARENT

You cannot win the heart of a wayward adolescent by being harsh towards them. You cannot win or reclaim them for Christ through cursing and insulting. You can only maintain hope through prayer and intercession for them. A wayward child needs love and compassion—just as any sinner. Treat them with the love of Christ. Speak kindly to them, and let them just not feel misunderstood and misjudged. Like the father of the prodigal son, be ready to receive them. Let them know your arms are open to receive them whenever they need help—someone to talk to or a shoulder to cry on.

Through my lived experiences, I encourage people to know that if they fall, they can rise again. I want to let you know that if your children are going wayward today, it is not the end of them. Allow them to go through their processes. This is what God could do with me. He takes what is rejected, and gone waste and prepares it to glorify Himself. And today, out of the darkness, I have risen into light. Out of the ashes, I have risen into the darkness of this world. I shine whenever I speak, and it touches hearts. Tears roll down my listeners' eyes, and that fulfills me. But until then, God would allow us to wonder in strange places—such as falling into the arms of an unfaithful lover.

CHAPTER 9

Love Doesn't Have to be Blind

Kofi and I had a complicated love for each other that kept our relationship going. Determined to remain lovers, we pushed through with our travel plan. Somewhere during the year 2001, the opportunity finally opened for me. With the help of his friend's girlfriend who was into the travel and tour business, I left Ghana for the UK. With resources from my rich lover, I was able to pay for her services as well as my ticket. I also was able to reserve some money to process Kofi's visa at a later time. Our plan to relocate to London was almost through.

I knew no one in London, but both Kofi, my boyfriend and Kofi my rich lover had cousins living and working there. We planned that I would lodge with Pokua, the cousin of my rich lover. He asked her to accommodate me until I could afford to rent a place of my own, and she gladly accepted to. When my lover's sister saw me for the first time at the Heathrow Airport where she came to pick me, she laughed so hard and remarked, "Oh my God! Such a young lady! And Kofi claims he loves you so very much and is going to marry you?

"Forget him, young lady. You are in the UK now. Build a life for yourself and move on in life. Don't let this man ruin your life!" She took me home and did as her brother had agreed with her, and supported me until I found stability. Those were some of the moments that I thought I had to sacrifice to get through in life! Those were memories of some of my hardest times! Being with someone for reasons other than love—because you know you don't love them.

By the time Kofi arrived in London, I had gotten settled in the home of Pokua, my rich lover's cousin in Mitchum, near Croydon. He took up temporal accommodation with his cousin at Elephant and Castle. He saved after working for a while and got a small place where I later joined him. We moved in together even when we hadn't yet married, but our relationship was both public and "official".

LOVE DOESN'T HAVE TO BE BLIND

We settled together happily, the whole of Ghana shut out—with all of the women trying to snatch my beloved from me. It felt like a new world altogether. But things soon took another sour turn. Unfortunately for us, but especially for me, Kofi's behaviour didn't change even after we had moved to London. He brought with him his character of chasing women. He went after girls on the streets of London, and one day I received hint of it. One of our neighbours we lived with in the same house told me told me he was seeing her.

At that time, I worked a night shift job. Kofi would drop me off at work, and go back home. But he would not go to bed alone. Instead, he would bring a girl to spend the night with. When I caught wind of it, I planned with my informant to return home immediately after he had dropped me off at work and left for the house by himself. It was the only way I could garner evidence to what I had heard. Indeed, after dropping me off one evening, I took a car back home, and behold, what I was told was true.

I became extremely angry—even frustrated. Out of my anger and frustration, I left the UK and came back to Ghana. Back in Ghana, I didn't give up seeking greener pastures outside the country.

I tried to secure a US visa, and succeeded! Before long, I was out of the country again.

I arrived in the USA in August of 2003. I was offered lodging by a friend in New Jersey. I soon settled for my first job as a Home Health Aide. After two months in New Jersey, I moved to Yonkers, New York, where I settled until 2021. I continued to work as a caregiver in NY until my friend could not continue to accommodate me. Fortunately for me, my next job would come with an accommodation. It was a live-in caregiver job in Connecticut, where I worked for a couple of years.

America is a great place. In America, I had total independence. I was by myself, lived the life of a single independent girl, self-sufficient because I had jobs I could do with my hands to earn me the money I needed.

But after being in America a little over a year, that is, towards the end of 2004, Kofi showed up and located me. Just like that, he resurfaced in my life out of nowhere, unexpectedly. Since we loved each other so much, it took little effort to rekindle our relationship. After listening to all that he had to go through to find me, I came to believe that he loved me indeed to have taken the risk he took to come to America in search of me.

After learning I had moved to the States, Kofi arranged with one of his former girlfriends with whom he cheated on me way back to help him travel to the US. This woman worked as a caterer. She and Kofi were seeing each other behind my back in the days we dated while in Ghana, and I had knowledge of their affair. Although she now lived in the US, she and Kofi were still in touch. Kofi approached her and had conversations about traveling to the States. His intention was to come look for me, but the only option was for her to extend invitations to him as a fiancé, and Kofi accepted. It was through this arrangement he secured travel documents to apply for his "fiancé" visa. To this woman, she and Kofi were going to get married when he arrives in America, but Kofi had a different intention, a secret intention. He was coming into America for love and marriage, but not to the woman whose name appeared on his official travel documents.

It had been three years since we went our separate ways, and having heard nothing from each other. At a time I least expected someone like him showing up in my life again, he reappeared, claiming he could not live without me. The last three years without me had been hell for him; he was just convinced I am his soul mate.

He sounded convincing, and circumstances in my own life seemed to suggest that he was right when he said we are soul mates. Somehow, I had remained single all the while I had been in America. I had only focused on working to earn money to support my mom and siblings. With lots of jobs available, I married my jobs and produced the money I wanted. It wasn't like Ghana anymore, where I would have to depend on a man to cushion me because my salary was meagre. Here, I made enough and had some to spare. The only thing that was missing in my life was a man I would settle down with. While I was financially independent, I still needed a man in my life. It was impossible that I would continue to work and never marry. But somehow, I had not been able to open up to any man. At the time Kofi found me, I was independent and comfortable, but I was also single.

Perhaps, he was the reason why I was afraid to open up to men who approached me for relationships. I was afraid I would fall into wrong arms like his. Whenever someone approached me and expressed interest, I resisted because I couldn't trust anyone after what I had been through at the hands of Kofi. I had the fear that perhaps these men approaching would act like him. I feared perhaps they even had wives and children back home in Ghana. They would thus take advantage of me. So I stayed true to myself. Never made up my mind to date anyone. But I wasn't waiting for Kofi. I wasn't expecting him back in my life. He was not the reason I was yet single.

Although I decided to pray about his proposal, and indeed, the entire incidence, my instincts prompted me to accept him. I wasn't sure whether to believe he was my soul mate or not. I remember assuming that God must have kept me single all this while for him. God knew He would bring him back, so He prevented me from falling in love again until Kofi's unexpected return. Somehow, the thought that Kofi's failure to find love must have arisen from his bad character didn't occur to me. Even if that could be true, I was too naïve to understand. So in spite of all the evidences that pointed to what I was to expect in a marital relationship with him, I went ahead to accept to marry him.

Another terrible mistake I made was settling on who to marry without talking to God about him in prayer. Here I am, choosing a husband for myself without asking God what He had for me or whether it was His will. I did not pray seriously about the relationship, I did not seek God's counsel. I did not wait to hear from God before going ahead to accept him into my life. All I saw was somebody who would give me extra money to add to my money and be able to do what I thought I had to do by myself.

One of my weaknesses was that I was not mature enough to understand what I was doing. Young people must know that maturity and wisdom are important for discerning the future of a relationship. That is why you would have to listen to your parents, mentors, pastors, counselors. I didn't listen to my mother and my many older office colleagues who saw the clear red flags and advised me against marrying him.

CHAPTER 10

A Price for the Glory

My mother became aware that Kofi and I had somehow ended up together again in the US. Just as before, and just as I expected, she remained displeased, even more disappointed now. How on earth this could happen? Like previously during our time in Ghana, she became furious when she learned about it. She had never been in favour of it, and still was not even now.

Convinced somehow, that Kofi and I were destined soul mates, I tried to convince my Mom that Kofi was a new person now. If he could put himself through all these in search of me, I will take him at his word and accept him back, and hope that indeed, he had changed over a new leaf. My mother refused to be persuaded. She objected, although I resisted her.

I was determined to go ahead with my plan to marry Kofi. But one morning, the legal American wife called. She accused me of snatching her husband. But when I confronted Kofi about cheating with his visa business friend, he denied. We had many fights over the phone. We argued lengthily.

According to her, she invited Kofi over to America because they agreed to marry. She did not do it to "help a friend" get the opportunity to travel into the US. She wanted to keep the man, who, on his part, merely wanted an opportunity to come into the US to meet and marry me. When I confronted Kofi, he claimed to have paid her for her "service". Additionally, she knew we were together back in Ghana. How she could claim to have married and invited him to the US was a wonder to me. It became a tag of war between us. But at this point, I had made up my mind to spend the rest of my life with Kofi. I decided I was not going to let anyone snatch him from me because he was mine. I became aggressive and did everything possible to have him. I'm not going to let you have my man. But she was much older than me, and hard to deal with. She fought me hard. But I insisted Kofi is my husband, I would marry him.

Our relationship was unstable as we drifted apart every now and then, making it an on and off relationship! Kofi could not secure his documents because his intention to not marry this lady was reveled before the documentation could be completed. She insisted she could only help him get his documents if he married her for real, and stopped seeing me. Amid these circumstances, I became pregnant with our first baby. When she realized that we had found each other and were together again, and that I was going to have a baby, she was not going to help Kofi complete the agreement they had had. Kofi left her without the documents towards the end of 2006. He shared my apartment and we cohabited at that time, and tried again to establish our relationship.

After moving in with me, we began to have babies. We had our oldest child, Rachael, in 2006, although we were not married. Time went by quickly, and in 2009, we had our 2nd child, Comfort, but lost her only a day after her birth due to an infection. We then had Sheila, our next daughter, in March of 2011. Exactly a year after Sheila, we had our son. Your guess is as good as mine. With that close gap between them, Sheila and David, aka Kofi Jr., are like twins, and that is what I call them—my twins.

But all the while we were not married. We finally had our traditional marriage May, 9th 2014. We had been together since 1996, and finally decided it was time to get married—after having three kids! Sometimes, I wonder why I did what I did, staying and having kids with a man I was not properly married to.

But eventually, members of Kofi's family went to perform the marriage rights on his behalf. But just about that time also, Kofi resumed his old lifestyle of womanizing. This time, to greater lengths. He went to the extent of staying away from home for long periods of time, return after a long absence, and immediately disappears again, and not be found for days. If I demanded explanations, it became a big issue between us. He had the guts to tell me, "This is how I am. I like women. You knew it before marrying me. Decide if you want to stay or leave."

As you would assume, it got me very worried. I felt foolish. I felt I had fallen. I began to regret very deeply. I had chosen a husband for myself without seeking God's opinion—and I am now regretting everything. I never stopped to hear from God, to be sure whether His hand was in the union or not. I relied on my own power and strength. I even turned a deaf ear to my mom's advice and objection. Now, who was I going to talk to? On whose shoulder was I going to cry? Certainly not my Mom I refused to listen to, and not the God I wasn't patient enough to wait upon. As time went on, my husband started coming into our matrimonial home with his women. And I was forbidden to ask questions or challenge him. He brought home his girlfriends to do what they please and leave at will. After all that I had gone through for him—at the hands of my Mom and at the hands of other women. After all the help I had offered him—to get him established in this city. After I had helped him to achieve making things better as we had hoped, he turned his back on me. He took it all for granted. But in the midst of it all, God was with me.

I felt really stuck, unable to move forward or retreat. I wondered what the right step to take was. I already had three little children; where would I take them if I wanted a divorce? So I become what? Single mother? Or I should be determined and face it till the end?

But these challenges started coming at a time I had established my faith in God so well, and I was gaining spiritual insights. I came to the realization that I was in a battle. I thus turned to praying as the only alternative. I reached out to my pastors and a small circle of friends with whom I usually pray. God, how did I come to fall into this big problem? God revealed to me that all of what I was going through was as a result of His calling on my life. "I am going to teach you lessons through your marriage. I want you to stand firm and watch my glory unfold. In the end, you will understand why I, the Lord permitted it. Not that I have not seen what you are going through. Not that I don't have power to rescue you from this terrible marriage or give you a better one. I even have power to change your husband. 'The heart of the king is in the hand of the Lord.' But I have chosen this man as my vessel for teaching you lessons to prepare you to strengthen women."

In all of this, I did everything to maintain a peaceful home. I remained humble in the midst of the chaos, and performed my duties as a wife—cooked, washed, cleaned—everything, even though my husband never appreciated them. Our relationship so severed that we lived a disunited life—as though in different worlds.

At one point, we decided to go our separate ways. After all these challenges in the marriage, we came to that conclusion between us. I decided I have had enough. It was time to move on. I was going to get a place of my own, and move out with my kids. But just about that period, Destiny, our surprise baby, was conceived. The night before that decision, he did everything he could to have an encounter with me, and four months later I found out that I was pregnant. At that time, I had evidence of his extra marital affairs in Ghana. We never spoke to each other from the night of the encounter and throughout my pregnancy, until my day of delivery.

One year after the delivery, he made the decision to go and follow his business in Ghana.

Sometimes I wonder why God would choose to give us a child in such a situation. Yet Destiny-Renee was destined to be born for a divine assignment and through us. Our relationship and marriage has stood the test of time indeed! We have been through so many battles, breakups, and concubines unlimited. We are traditionally still married, since the marriage hasn't been dissolved. He left me and the kids to embark on his business venture, and this has put a lot of strain on the relationship and the family.

CHAPTER 11

Seeking Advancement

One of the best things you can do at any point in time in your life is to advance yourself academically, spiritually, and career wise. You will stand to benefit immensely from it. It was one way I dealt with my marital challenges. However challenging the entire experience was, the excitement of being in school took my attention away from the problems of stress and broken-heartedness posed in my life by my marriage.

Indeed, when I got to America, I still possessed my passionate for education, although I wasn't in the position to put myself through school. At the appointed time, God ordained stability for me. I realized I could put myself back to school. It is a miracle that I found the opportunity to resume schooling in the midst of my marital challenges.

During the 2014 year period, I decided it was time to upgrade myself academically. I enrolled at Westchester Community College to pursue an Associate Degree in Social Sciences and Substance Abuse Counseling.

After the registration, I was examined. My transcripts from Ghana were evaluated and found to be not equivalent to the US High School degree which should qualify me to enter college and pursue a first degree programme. I enquired what I needed to do, and I was made to first take some GED classes with courses to prepare me for the GED certificate. Taking the courses brought my SSSCE certificate to their diploma level, and my performance was pretty good.

At the beginning, my dream was to become a nurse in the short-term; the bigger goal would then be to become the doctor I had always wanted to be. I entered the college to purse an associate degree in Social Science. When I entered the nursing program, I knew I was preparing for a nursing career, and I was going to function in the "helping" field. I was going to be someone who will touch lives, and I was excited about it.

I was excited because I love to serve. I serve without complaining. I have a naturally empathetic heart and I strive to bring out the best in others. They are traits of my father I carry: humility and kindness of heart.

Actually, both my parents possess that quality. So I have always loved to help people; that is my nature. I want to bring consolation to people. I thought, therefore, that nursing was the field where I could get the opportunity to put these traits to use. But in the process of my preparation for my nursing career, I got stack and didn't know why. It came to light that God had a different plan for me, but it wasn't in the area of medicine, my childhood dream.

It happened that as part of the requirement of my Nursing Assistant programme, I was to undertake internships as a Nursing Assistant. During the internship, I attended to patients at the bedside at night. Part of our duty as Nursing Assistants was to change patients' clothes in the night, and provide bedside care. I observed that the Nurses attended to this task in so much haste. When they get to a patient, they hurriedly remove their old cloth, replace them with a new one, and move to the next patient as quickly as they could. They didn't bother to communicate with them; they just did their job strictly.

I observed—heartbroken—because I felt that some of them needed extra care and gentleness to handle. What if they had some pain for which reason extra care was required in handling them? I won't take the way they handled these poor patients. Human beings shouldn't be treated like dead bodies!

What happens to greeting someone when you enter their home or room? What happens to exchanging pleasantries and knowing how one is faring? That is my custom, naturally. When I enter a house, I want to greet it, I want to find out how its inhabitants are doing. I want to treat people as humans, instead of just counting how many patients I have to finish with and move to the next thing. That was how I approached the work. I was very nice to the patients. "Hello, good morning, Darryl. How are you today and how was your night?" I would say upon reaching a patient's bed.

But the nurses began to be upset with me for taking time to greet and enquire about how patients were doing. I was taking time to be nice to people and it was delaying their work. The senior nurse came to me one day and said, "You have time for everybody's business? Then nursing is not your job. You should have to be a social worker—if you want to take all the time in the world to be with one person. We're not here to do that. We're here to change patients and leave. It is not our business how anybody doing!"

It sounded harsh, but I was hard-hit by those words. "No, I don't just want to change people and leave them in their state? When some of them are emotional and I can tell just by looking into their faces! They need somebody to talk to for a moment; somebody to tell them that everything is going to be OK. And you can't spare a minute of your time because you are rushing. Then this indeed is not my job!"

I began to ponder the words of the senior nurse as the days went by. "You have time for everybody? Then nursing is not your job. Be a social worker." Lying in my room one day, it was as though God was revealing the Social Work to me. But I had no idea what a job in the Social Work field was all about. It was a totally new phenomenon to me.

When I was growing up in Ghana, especially during my time back in the 90s, I never knew a single person who ever said they were going to complete school and become a Social Worker. I knew about the Social Welfare but wasn't sure whatever they existed for. Was the department even functioning? I had never even set eyes on the department building. It was when the family moved to live around Madina that I learned of something called Social Welfare. They have their office around Madina, and it was a very popular location. But as to whether they were supporting the community, the youth, the needy, or the homeless, I had no idea.

I reached for my cell phone and googled. Google gave me sufficient information about Social Work. What it entails, their criteria of work, what it took to become a social worker—a whole lot. I read all about it online, taking note of the core values and principles of the profession, and impressed myself. This is what I want to be. That person who reaches out to you in your broken state. That person who reaches out and helps you out of your darkness—gradually, little by little, step by step. That person who does not come to judge and condemn you and remind you of what fool you've made of yourself. That person who comes to support you with their resources until you reach the end of your tunnel where there is light.

I felt God manifesting Himself and saying, "Mary, you are born for this. You are a change agent. I have made you my mouth piece to speak for change for the less-privileged and the marginalized in society. So you have to become a Social Worker." After a long deliberation, I came to the conviction that Social Work was my calling. It is the field I wanted to be found making impact. And I would choose it a thousand times over.

But at this time also, not only had I advanced in age, but I had also gone a long way in my current academic pursuit. I had advanced in my studies and in the nursing field. Indeed, my counselors were surprised that with just two semesters to go, I had decided to switch from Nursing to Social Work. They wondered what had triggered my decision when I had only two semesters to complete the current programme and graduate. When they realized I was resolute in my decision to switch after I told them I wasn't interested in becoming a nurse, and that Social Work was my calling, they offered suggestions on how to arrive at my goal.

With about 7 courses in the human services field to complete the associate degree at the time I was transitioning into the Social Work field, my counselors advised me to finish the classes for the associate in Social Science before adding other classes that would prepare me for the degree to enter into Social Work. I complied with their counsel. In the end, I had two degrees, though that was not my initial plan. In two semesters, I was able to finish up all the classes, to give me the Social Work degree to attach to what I was originally in school for.

My story should teach you that it is important that you seize opportunities to grow or sharpen your skills and expertise. Apart from keeping you busy and hence diverting your mind from what is ensuing in your marriage, going back to school to get an advanced degree or learning a trade or taking a course to develop your skills will enhance your career and finances. That, predominantly, should be your goal of advancing academically. Getting advanced degrees positioned me to earn more income to meet my responsibilities—especially as a single mother of four.

In some cases also, your not growing and advancing socially and finically and contributing to your marriage can give room for your husband to take advantage of you. In my case, going back to school did more than upgrade me academically and advancing my career. It practically led me to discover my purpose in life, my calling. God called me to go into the social work field through circumstances relating to my seeking academic advancement. I discovered after resuming school that I was do develop and build a career in Social Work. I don't know what you would discover along the path to seeking advancement for your life. But I do know it will be worth the efforts, and you won't regrets your actions.

Up until then, I had not sought the face of God concerning what to do with my life. And thus, I was not doing what He wanted me to do. God made me understood that I was pursuing my own plans, and that I choose to go into nursing by my own will. I didn't know, I hadn't considered, but God had a different career plan for me.

CHAPTER 12

God's Master Plan

I enrolled back in school in the midst of all the turmoil in my marriage. When I saw the need, as well as the opportunity, I did not allow the challenges in my marriage to hinder me. Little by little, crying and trying, I pushed towards accomplishing my academic goals.

I was privileged to get a lot of scholarships to complete my Social Science program at Westchester Community College. By the grace of God, I excelled, and graduated with honours, and became a member of Phi Theta Kappa.

I went on to complete a Bachelor's degree in Social Work at Mercy College, Dobbs Ferry, NY, where I would also graduate with high honor, and became a member of Phi Alpha Honors Society, before proceeding to New York University (NYU). I was just fortunate to get admission into the NYU. The NYU is one of the most prestigious university colleges in New York City and New York as a whole. Getting admission into that college was a rare opportunity for someone like me. Knowing my poor background—coming from parents like I had, I could in no way be considered amongst people being selected to come to the US—and to study in the US—and in institutions like the prestigious NYU, but for grace. NYU is a top school; and admission into it competitive. Out of my numerous colleagues with whom I completed Westchester Community College, Valhalla, and Mercy College, in Dobbs Ferry, only three of us ventured into NYU—and I was the only Black.

If not for grace, what would be the business of a girl from a poor background like me in NYU? Talk less of even pursuing a program at the master's level! At the time I entered the NYU, I was a mother of three kids. At the same time, my marriage was falling apart. I was brokenhearted, experiencing pain upon pain.

I never got the support my academic endeavours would have enjoyed from a spouse. When I graduated, friends and members of my church graced the occasion, but my husband did not show up. When we came home to have the graduation party, he came in and dressed up and left me and the children and our guests. Embarrassing as that was, it became evident to the entire world that my husband took me for nothing. He was a husband who didn't have an iota of respect for his wife, nor care about my achievements.

But in all of it, God gave me great patience and courage and strength. He reminded me of where He had taken me from—from when I was only a kid on the streets of 37, suffering and growing through hardship. He didn't forsake me, and didn't leave me into the hands of the devil. When I fell terribly ill and could have died, He didn't allow the illness to take my life. Those times I used to rove in the late nights, and could have fallen into traps of death, rape and destruction, He rescued me from it all. He kept me save from rapists and evil in all its other forms. This is not the time to hand me into the hands of the devil. Not after bringing me this far—into America and into a marriage. He didn't bring me here to disgrace me.

It was as though God wanted to say, "Ama, I did not intentionally let you go through this marital challenges to hurt you. Instead, it was a stage I was using to prepare you for your calling and audience. I have called you to a ministry to women who are abused and rejected. Women who have no hope, or whose hope in marriage is gone—because, like you, they are despised by their husbands. Women who are shedding tears every day in their marriages. I have called you to these, which is why I have allowed your life to go down this lane.

Many times, I took a careful consideration of myself. I wanted to be sure everything was fine on my part. I wanted to be sure I didn't do anything to have brought these calamities upon me. I wanted to be sure I was truly who I thought I was. I took a careful consideration. I concluded that I was not the kind of woman who deserved this treatment. I was well raised. I know how to make a home. I am humble. I am intelligent and learned, but humble to the point of doing everything a wife should do, to the amazement of other people who know us. People even use me as an example of a model wife. They reference me to their daughters and daughters-in-law. Yet the man who was lucky to have this kind of wife took me for granted. Unknowingly, it was as a result of the calling upon my life. It was all to prepare me for my calling.

The moment you discover the reason behind a thing, relief comes. Things we do not understand tend to appear complex and mysterious. When

I discovered why I was going through these things, I had peace. It wasn't my fault: I was not a bad wife; I was not ugly and unattractive. Also, the moment I found out why these things had to happen in my life, I found my calling. I found my calling the moment it hit me—that aha moment—when it dawned on me why all these were happening. Oh my God! Mary, this is why! This is why! This is the reason I have been so graciously broken. This is why my marriage had become so bitter, so devoid of joy, openness and trust. I desired a man who would love me just the way I would love him, to have a life with. A humble and God-loving man, who will foster my growth in the Lord. I wanted a man so descent that there will be no need for a third party to know about what is going on in our marriage. I did not get it, regardless of what I did or how much I put into the relationship. I found out that God had other intentions for my marriage. He would use it to break me, not to destroy me, but to bring out the best version of me—and to bring out His purpose in me.

One reason I can say so is also because, it was during this period of my life that my passion for God and for His work and Kingdom intensified. I came to realize that it was only God that had never let me down. As for the man I thought I loved so much, the man I thought I should sacrifice everything to enjoy the future with, the least said the better. All I had left was God; I had only God to hold on to. As my passion for the things of God experienced that great growth, I prayed like never before, studied the Word of God more, and served God and the church. I became totally sold out to God and His business. The church became a home to my children and me. It was the only place we could be found in the whole of the United States, beside home or office. I could not be found at the club or party like the big weekend parties people throng. I do socialize, but by the grace of God, I am not addicted to the things of the world. The first and likely place you would find me then was the church—with my children. I am very aware of my surroundings and the people I associate with. I learned how to guard my tongue and take my battles to God in prayer. And when I found myself in these circumstances, I prayed and prayed and prayed and prayed.

I took my education very seriously, and didn't play with my studies at all. I said to myself, they can take my man from me, but they cannot take my wisdom and my God-given abilities from me. You can have my man, but as for me, I give myself up for the Master's use. I focused on my studies. I knew that someday, God would plant me in great place to glorify Him. I knew that someday, He will lift me high. That is why I took seriously the opportunities I had to further my education, giving it my all. I pushed so hard, and by grace, I finished my Bachelor's and Master's.

As a college—and later graduate student, I enjoyed tremendous blessings from the Lord. He blessed me with divine knowledge, wisdom and understanding. I was one of the strongest in my class. Not because I was too smart, of course. When I left SSS, I went into selling for so long, engaging in activities that didn't bother on reading or training my brain. I didn't even know how come I still excelled so much academically.

God has promised us He will take us to the Promised Land. What He didn't tell us is the struggles we have to endure through the wilderness. In between the land of slavery and the Promised Land there is a wilderness. You will get to the Promised Land as God has promised, but you cannot avoid the challenging journey through the wilderness. What did I not go through? Prolonged wilderness experience? At every step of my progress, I had to be crushed and broken. But through it, He molded me into different forms, and I always came out better until I was molded into the product He fully desired me

to be. What I became after each and every season of crushing and breaking always superseded the previous. Every day, He did new things with me that were far beyond understanding. And little by little, step by step, the child from the poor background came to have a degree, and went on to have a Masters—even through tragedy and pain. And now a beautiful career in sync with God's purpose for creating me. What fulfilment!
I consider myself a complete product of the grace of God. It is not out of my own wisdom or knowledge. It is not because of the opportunities the nation of America gave me. It is not because today I have become a psychotherapist, sitting in an own office and diagnosing patients and giving them labels of crises they go through. It is not because today I am a renowned Social Worker, and doing God's work alongside. It is not because God has given me the grace to speak into microphones to large crowds and bring them counseling. It is purely out of grace.

Above all, He has turned my story and my mistakes into a blessing. He has given me a ministry out of it. And you can believe God for a similar experience. You can patiently wait upon Him to give you beauty for your ashes.

CHAPTER 13

Evolve Again, Woman

Anyone who reads or listens to my story may come to one of two conclusions. I made foolish mistakes, but God used them for His glory. Or, God took me on a path I would have least opted for, to unveil and fulfill His purpose in me.

To someone reading my story, I fell into all this as a result of my own making. To them, I brought these troubles upon myself through my own mistakes. Those who think so could be right. We all make mistakes in life. The prodigal son made his mistakes. David made his mistake of committing adultery with the wife of Uriah. Peter denied Jesus. I made my mistakes, too. I am human. I admit that I could have avoided it all, perhaps, by not marrying a man who showed me his real character again and again long before

I decided to tie the knot with him. But even if they are the result of my own mistakes, God has turned them around for His glory. Just as He turned David's mistake into Solomon, the wisest and most magnificent of kings. Even the prodigal son came back home to a great party. And Peter received restoration.

I don't know what mistakes you have made in life. But I want you to believe that God can use your mistakes to bless generations. He can heal your broken-heart, liberate you from your bondage, comfort you in your mourning, give you beauty for ashes and turn your shame into glory.

There were times I looked back with regrets for taking up employment at Asare Original Pay All, where I met my husband. God! Had it not been so, I'd probably have met someone else—a nice man with whom I will have a wonderful life, and I surely had one who would have died for me.

But what I have become today also convinces me that God may have taken me down this path to prepare me for my calling. Today, when I teach women, speak to women or counsel women, I easily identify with their struggles when they talk about them. When I listen to them, I hear stories similar to mine, and I relate to them easily because I have been through them, too. God took me through them for this purpose. He wasn't punishing me, He was preparing me for such an assignment as this.

When we encounter people who are going through what we have been through before, it is easier to identify with them. It is easier to help them. Our responses to them are swifter, and we are less critical and judgmental of them. God does not always need to take us through terrible experiences to prepare us, but when He does, the results are amazing. So He sometimes uses that approach to prepare vessels He intends to use (2 Corinthians 1:3–4). It is the path He chose to walk me through for the ministry He had called me to. Having come to the understanding that God meant well for me in all this, I hold no grudge towards my husband for what he put me through, however gross his actions were, and however painful, embarrassing, agonizing, traumatic the experience was for me. Till today—even this moment I am writing, I am able to look him in the face and say, "Papa Kofi, thank you for everything you took me through". At first, I was angry and I resented him for what he did to me. But when God opened my eyes to its connectedness to my calling, I changed my perspective. Now I have gratitude, instead, in my heart—to him, to God, for everything. I am thankful to him for "availing himself" to be used by God to teach me the things I needed to know to be ready and prepared for the purpose of God for me. "So, yes, Gentleman, I don't hate you. I thank God for you. You have been very instrumental in shaping me. You have been my textbook—the source of the lessons I write on abuse. They come to me as natural and as the truth. I thank you for giving me that experience. For this, I honor you."

When I say things like that, he would look quietly at me, not sure what exactly I am trying to point out. He doesn't understand the angle I'm coming from.

What is the lesson here for you, dear reader? What do you take out this story? Simple lesson is, God can deliver you from whatever you're going through in your marriage, if you hold on to Him firmly. If you are being mocked and laughed at because of your marital problems, God can glorify you through it. Someday, your cup will run over, because that is what He has done with me. Today, God has brought under my feet those who were leading me in their marriages. Mary Ama Zuruba—the woman who was rejected and taken for granted.

EVOLVE AGAIN, WOMAN

After I completed all the "training" God wanted to take me through, He said, "Ama, I have just given you wings. You are about to soar like an eagle and never get tired. You are going to soar and all eyes will see what I have done with you. What ears have not heard is what I am doing in your life, and what eyes have not seen, I am yet to do. You are still a work in progress. I am not done with you, Ama."

Now, I am a free woman, serving God to the best of my ability. Serving society, touching mankind, providing encouragement and support to the broken woman.

Speaking from a wealth of personal experience, I am able to tell the broken woman, "Woman, you will evolve again." "Woman, there is a greater woman in you." The fact that you were rejected in your marriage does not end your story. Your marriage does not define you or what God has called you to be. Arise and give glory to God. Rise from your weakness, rise from your brokenness. Speaking from experience too, I can counsel young women who are now preparing to enter into marriage to learn from me by praying for the leading of God. Let God lead you. Pray concerning your marriage and commit your ways to the Lord, so that He will hold your hand

and take you through. If, after you have prayed and done all you should do as a child of God, the marriage continues to face challenges, don't despair; don't be moved. Lift up your face to the Lord Jesus. He knows what He is about. He is up to something good. He will not leave you nor forsake you. Victory will be yours in the end.

Whoever knew me in America knew I was crying in my marriage. I am the woman who never saw a single joy in my marriage. The young woman who went through thick and thin during childhood, looked forward to comfort in marriage, but got disappointed. I put all my hope in a man—because I had no father or elder brother. But instead of caring and consoling, he betrayed. As much as his family was supportive of me, it was tough. Sometimes I asked God, "Lord, why? I give up." But the Holy Spirit would stir me up and bring me into remembrance—where He took me from and where He has brought me—and I would be encouraged.

When I developed passion for prayer and resorted to praying intensely, my husband would ask me, "So you have nothing doing in this world except making noise in the name of praying? Is church all you know to do? No partying, no discoing, no clubbing? See how people are enjoying life in

EVOLVE AGAIN, WOMAN

America—your fellow women. And all you do is pray?" Indeed when I got to the US, I became a totally changed person. Unlike when I was in Ghana and thought I didn't have what it took to make it, things were different in America. In Ghana, I depended on wealthy men, and they decided where I spent my time and what I did. If they wanted me to spend time with them hanging out—at clubs, restaurants and beaches, I yielded, because their money spoke. But in America, I was, by the grace of God, in a place where I could work with my own hands and earn a living. So I killed myself for money. I lost every interest in all worldliness—partying, holidaying, spending time hanging out.

So it was true. That used to be our lifestyle back in Ghana when we first met. But after I settled in the US, and gotten married to him, I was arrested by God. I run away from the things of the world. Additionally, my job never allowed me time to do some of these things. So I didn't attend occasions such as funerals, and other social gathering as much. But as for all worldly things, I thank the Lord for separating me from them, and making me interested in only what pertains to His Kingdom. And because He doesn't disappoint those who trust in Him, He hasn't let me down. He has blessed me and made me great. But I paid dearly for my loss of interest in them: it cost me my marriage.

When my husband complained about me—and even left me to follow other women, people who hadn't met me yet—including his girlfriends, thought I was some unattractive, "uncivilized" girl. But when they see me, they get surprised. "You have a beautiful wife and you are doing all this?" "Oh, she doesn't like going out. Even funerals, she doesn't attend. Every day she wakes up, all she does is pray in tongues—she and her children." Then people would remark, "You're a beautiful girl. But why don't you go out and have a little fun?"

What both they and my husband refused to understand is that, life is not meant to be a roller-coaster. It is not meant to be sweet or fun throughout. Things change. Circumstances change. People change. Everyone should expect that the people in our lives—our spouses, children and relatives, colleague workers and friends may become new versions of themselves. They may go through experiences that leave them changed in their way of thinking and analyzing things and in their beliefs and convictions. It is up to us to handle their new versions.

There are things we all don't like about ourselves — height, complexion, stature, or even race. But we have to learn to live with them because we cannot change them. Marriage is sometimes like that. We have to learn to live with the choices we make.

When we make our choice of a spouse, we are not able to guarantee that it'll give us beautiful kids. We are able to guarantee that they will remain who they were when we married them — attractive, sane, or healthy. We cannot even guarantee their spirituality. But no one ever threw their children away because they were not cute. Similarly, the outcome of the marriage itself is something we have to learn to live with. After all, we vowed for better or for worse.

A spouse should thus learn to handle the change that occurred to me and be able to patiently endure. God will not tempt us beyond what we are able to contain (1 Corinthians 10:3). It means nothing can go so wrong in our marriage that we cannot bear. Don't run away from your family when you encounter challenges. Don't compromise your faith because of the outcome of your marriage. Stand firm. Try to understand your spouse. Be empathic. Be patient. Work things out.

CHAPTER 14

The Cost of Greatness

Every strong and successful person out there has a story. Those who know my marital struggles ask how I survived. I tell them it was the grace of God. I have come to understand that God was using what outsiders saw to be negative in my marriage, and what they saw to be tormenting me, to prepare me.

At a point, my mom and friends and loved ones were so deeply concerned about me. They feared something might happen to me. They cried bitterly and lost heart. But I told them to not fight the battle for me. I told them God was at work. I understood that it was my calling and my destiny. I understood what God is doing. If you want to fight it for me, you will fight endlessly. You will be fighting a lost battle. I knew how to fight my battle—on my knees in prayer. "You are too soft; you are too calm." "You're sitting there and holding on to the Word of God, and watching your husband mistreat you." But I tell them, "The battle is not mine to fight. God knows what He is doing."

There were times he mistreated me so much, and the next day at work, the first client to sit at my desk for counseling shares their story, and it is as if they are telling my story instead. It is as if they lived with me in my matrimonial home—and hence knew everything happening there. Sometimes, I sit at my desk and I have to comport myself to avoid breaking down because of the trauma that my fellow woman sitting opposite me is talking about, and seeking my help about in counseling. But I am myself going through the same thing. It is how God sometimes speaks to me when I'm in my chair counselling. "Ama, this is what happened to you yesterday. So now, I need you to empower this woman, because I have given the grace to you."

Sometimes, when I speak to people or to my patients or clients, I don't know where I get the words from. The Holy Spirit speaks through me. When I finished talking and was asked to repeat myself, I would not be able to because the flow had come from the Holy Spirit. Sometimes too, when I counsel them, they remark, "Impressive! You have so much wisdom. I find peace and hope in your speech." But all I do when they leave my office is to lock my door and cry.

I pray and hope that if you are going through any challenge in life, you will learn to be still and know that there is God.

As a social worker, I would advise that if you're dealing with ABUSE, don't wait till it is too late. Don't let someone take your life. If a man is abusing you, the fact that you should pray, and ask God to visit your marriage does not mean stay in that marriage, and in that abuse, and die. One thing that is disturbing is that unfortunately, a lot of women and children of God pay the ultimate price of losing their life because they remain holding on to certain age-old philosophies. "God hates divorce. Therefore, a Christian should not divorce." Then they try to endure, hoping that God will fix things. But God has given you wisdom. If you are close to God enough in your relationship with Him, you will acknowledge that you cannot love your neighbour more than yourself. Don't put their welfare ahead of yours by remaining in the abuse until it is too late. You should withdraw yourself from any situation that is a threat to your life or survival.

Withdraw to preserve your life. If you reach a point where your life is threatened, wake up. I struggled emotionally but managed to garner the strength to resist what the world was throwing at me because I had the presence of God dwelling in me. I engaged myself in a positive way and I learned to look at the good in the bad. I usually left for our church premises with my children to spend time. Find a place of safety for yourself, go on a girls' vacation trip to places, like I did to Purto Rico with my spiritual sisters. Have some positive and spiritual associations.

Fortunately for me, I did not get to the point where I was turned into a punching bag, or physically abused or pushed around. But I plead with you, if you are going through physical or even emotional abuse and you cannot contain it, I implore you to seek help. Don't live in an abusive marriage and let it kill you. Seek help if you are depressed and broken. There is no shame in seeking help. I treat a lot of women of God. I talk to a lot of pastors' wives going through their own stuff. There's nothing wrong with it. Be willing to talk it out with someone you can trust.

Surround yourself with positive people—people who will guide you, lead you, pray with you and empower you. Not negative people, who could

THE COST OF GREATNESS

use what you tell them about you against you. Indeed, don't be too quick to give information about yourself and what you're going through to other people. The less your enemies—or people in general—know about you, the better.

There is grace for everyone out there to endure difficult times. Pray that if there is any lessons in the trajectory of your marriage, God will reveal it to you. When God reveals it to you, you will realize why you're going through them. You will also realize the need to learn to pray more and hold on.

No one can be great unless it costs them something. Unless they go through some transformation in their life. I have been through mine. I am not an advocate for women or a voice for women because I am smarter or eloquent. Neither did it just come to me. I paid a price for it. I went through the process. It cost me a lot—my own happiness and joy in marriage—all just for you. Just so that you will hear my story.

Don't kill yourself because a man doesn't love you or because a man has rejected you. Focus your energies on working on yourself, on advancing yourself, on empowering yourself. Do things that make you happy. Build a future for yourself. Improve yourself through education. Grow in your profession or career. What do you want in life? What makes you happy? Your happiness is not in anybody's hands. The power to change your situation lies within you; use it. Open up and let God have His way in your life. Keep yourself busy. Pray, advance and remain humble. God will see you through.

I own the good and the bad in my marriage. I was supposed to make those mistakes. I wasn't supposed to enter the marriage in the first place. But I did—to my own detriment, therefore I own it. I am not ashamed of it. If you are going through the same thing and you think that you have sinned and don't know what to do about it, I am here to teach you how I handled mine, so you could learn from me. Confess your sins and God will forgive you. The trauma from my childhood contributed so much to the outcome of my marriage. It made me hold on to what I was not supposed to hold on to. If you are a mother, try to not transfer the trauma you're going through to your child. Seek help for yourself. Own the good—and the bad. It is your story.

Marital problems such as mine can be distressing. If you been through it before, you would never wish it for anybody. I do not wish for anybody—

whether a man or a woman, to go through the kind of issues that fraught my marriage. I do not want anybody to end up like me. I am writing this book to advise everyone to open their eyes to every red flag before making a decision. Remember how many red flags I ignored. Don't repeat my mistakes. All of the pain I had to endure would have been avoided if only I had paid heed to these red flags—my mother's voice, and more so, Kofi's infidelity. Be matured before entering into any relationship.

Avoid insecurity as a basis for getting married. In other words, don't marry for security. Learn to love yourself. Learn to believe in yourself. God is on your side. Even in the midst of my challenges, I had God's assurance. He is our security. There is nothing to fear because God is on our side. Whether or not we have money, education, connections or important figures in our lives, what is the most important is having God on your side.

EPILOGUE

During the time my mother traded along one of the streets within the 37 Military Hospital premises, a lot of events occurred. Over the period, the hospital underwent different stages of refurbishments and other infrastructural developments. To pave way for some of these developments, a lot of restructuring took place. A Singles Quarters block that housed young unmarried soldiers was converted into a hostel for the female nursing students of the hospital's nursing training college. At one point, the traders along the stretch of road by which my mom's shed was located were prohibited from selling there. A wall was erected between that road and the barracks. Mom was restricted to selling only within the barracks, right by the nursing hostel. During that 18 year period I lived at the barracks, I really saw the hospital transform in so many ways. It's been many years since I last stepped foot there, but even today, improvements and other forms of physical developments are still taking place in this hospital.

When I reflect over my life today, I am inclined to liken it to the 37 Military Hospital. God has transformed my life the way the 37 Military Hospital environment transformed right before my eyes. I am certain that after reading my story, you are better convinced that my life is, indeed, a definition of grace as I pointed out in the introduction. God has taken me through a lot of challenges, but He has also done me a lot of good. He has brought me to the realization that when He has something good for you, and if His call is upon your life, you will go through a lot in life, but come out victorious. People will underestimate you, judge you, talk behind your back. You will go through suffering as I have. My God! I've been through so much; I have suffered a lot in life. But today, I realize it was to uncover His purpose for my life.

I have had to struggle at every stage of my life—from my childhood to my youth. But at every stage, God saw me through—and it was because of His calling upon my life. I have had to go

EPILOGUE

through all those stages and arrive at this point in my life as a therapist, as a social worker, and as a woman of God so that I could relate naturally to everyone in any of these stages in their own life. Indeed, there is no level of life stage I cannot identify with. I have seen it all, I have been through it all, I have lived through it all.

During my advanced education in the US, I became very good at what I did. I excelled in my papers and stood out in every project that I did. My secret was that I was not drawing content from textbooks. I was drawing from my own experiences. When I write about an abandoned child, a child struggling, or a child afraid in life, I wrote from my own perspectives, and my own lived experiences. When we talk about a widow, a broken woman, a broken child, a broken man even, I relate with them all owing to what I have been through with my mother and my family. My lived experiences became my strength—academically and professionally.

He taught me that, as a homeless child sleeping by the wayside, if He didn't have any good thing in store for me, He wouldn't have allowed day and night to break and fall upon me. A child suffering to feed should have no fear about their dreams for a better tomorrow. You can become what your heart tells you that you will become. I know you have a dream: to become a nurse, teacher, doctor, pastor, businessman—whatever. Yet everything around you today, and your position in life may only tell you that you cannot achieve those dreams. I want to let you know that you don't have to be afraid, for God is with you. If He has said anything about you, He will do it. If He has brought me this far according His will, I want a child reading my story today, or an elderly person that will hear my message to not be discouraged.

Let my story inspire you to have faith. Let it give you hope and encourage you through your storms and your wilderness. Remember all that I have been through until now. I was the child that was once homeless. The child that once went to school with an empty chop box, too poor to afford textbooks or pay registration fee. Today I am "somebody"—living in the US of all places, with a Master's degree, looking to enter a PhD, to soon become Dr. Mary Ama Zuruba. Today, I live in a big house in America. Not a small house, but a mansion—far beyond comprehension.

Anytime I think about my life, Tasha Cobbs Leonard's Gracefully Broken says it all for me. I am the woman who has been gracefully, graciously

EPILOGUE

and beautifully broken. Indeed, God does not break you to destroy you. God has taught me that when we go through difficult times, it is not because He has forsaken us. Rather, it is because He is preparing us for our next level.

I love my story; I love what I have been through in life, although there were times I questioned and challenged God about so many things. Why did my father die so early? You know there was no one to take care of us; why did you take him? God why? But I learned that through it all, He never gave up on me. I have come to understand why, and today, glory be to God that I do not challenge any situation or changes that has happened in my life. God has taught me these lessons through the challenge.

God has been faithful to my mom too. The widow who was selling roasted maize and plantain by the roadside, nicknamed kayayo, because she was always running around with dirty feet and slippers. To the glory of God, my mother is living in America; a country of which she is a citizen. The child who had once gone wayward, today, through me, my Mom is a US citizen. People marvel when they see it. They marvel that God could lift a woman from such a background to such glory. And I, the Mary who went to Krobo Girls with an empty chop box always, who followed the husband of another woman—see what the Lord has done with me. The girl who hawked broflot, sweet bud, water, oranges, tangerine, maize, plantain on the streets of Accra, sleeping in the open after my father's death. After all the suffering, I am living in the US today, treating people and offering them encouragement. Today, I am God's messenger to thousands, God having put His message in my mouth.

I urge parents whose children seem to be going wayward to commit to praying and interceding for them, as God prepares them. When the time is up, He will transform them for His purpose. They may have gone wayward and spoilt, but leave them to God. They will crush and return. If only you have sown a good seed in them.

To you, my reader who thinks that you don't have what it takes to accomplish your goals in life, God says, "I have called you by your name…"; don't be afraid. The God who created you will never leave you nor forsake you. Glory be to God; He never disappoints. He will provide for you. Because He had something good for me, He placed people in every stage of my life to intercept mw, to support me, to shield me, to

EPILOGUE

protect me, to guide me. He can do same for you. Maybe you have put all your hope in God, but still things are not going as you wish. Remember God works according to times and seasons, so be patient. Keep holding on to him. Don't be moved in the midst of the storms. Don't be shaken. Don't be afraid. Don't be moved by what your eyes see today. Trust God and hold firmly to Him. He cannot forget you.

It is my prayer that my testimony will encourage you through your challenging moments—as a poor student or parent who doesn't know where your next meal is going to come from; as a crying, hopeless orphan, who doesn't know what to do with your life; as a child that is lost and afraid; as a fallen believer or one time successful career women or as a jobless husband. If God can feed the birds of the air through the seasons, then do not be afraid no matter your current conditions.

Made in the USA
Columbia, SC
07 May 2024

a9c1282f-734b-406f-bec9-d0474054e387R01